This book is dedicated to my children Sarah and Jacob. Because they fill my life with page after page of strength, faith, happiness, solidarity, hope and laughter. Never in my life have I had a team like this. Thank you babies. I'm so thankful that you're mine. I'm so thankful that I'm yours.

1.2.3.

D1526809

Contents

CHAPTER ONE

Everything does not happen for a reason

I 'm not grateful for it.

And I'm not EVER going to be.

I know.

We're all supposed to be grateful for everything, aren't we. Grateful and thankful, especially for the really bad stuff. It seems as if the worse it is, the more you're supposed to appreciate it. Like that is the true sign of a well-balanced person. For me, that's absolute nonsense; a big fat NO. I'm not grateful for this.

And another one I'm never going to agree with either is that everything happens for a reason. That?! Is <u>absolute</u> nonsense. Bad things happen sometimes, and you can survive it and you can thrive after it and that doesn't mean that you have to be grateful for it. I have so many times and people and places I am grateful for; beautiful memories that make up my life of gratitude. But this? I'm not grateful for this. I'm not and I'm not going to be.

Not Ever.

CHAPTER TWO

When I could hold their hands

When I was first diagnosed I ...well, I was going to tell a quick story about a celebrity who has multiple sclerosis and something she said in an interview that made my jaw drop and my heart sing with validation. But that will have to come later. It couldn't have been when I was first diagnosed because I remember so little from that time. Before the diagnosis. Before and after the park collapse. So much blurs together. What do I remember?

I remember March 31st, giving the kids the last of the eggs for breakfast and deciding to head to A&P later and get some groceries; I wasn't that hungry then anyway. And we had plans right after breakfast to walk to the park to meet my best friend, Andrea.

We walked past the yellow daffodils I planted when I bought my house, and the mint that I didn't plant, but runs wild... we went around the corner, and we held hands as we crossed the street.

"Hand train!" And I put both hands out to my side. They know what it means. They laugh as they each grab a hand and I say, "We look to the left!" They do. "We look to the right!" They do. We all decide it's all clear and we cross the street, excitedly talking about our trip. TEN DAYS! It's only ten days away. We're going to Turks and Caicos -the Beaches Resort. We've been there before, and we love it so much. It's one of those all-inclusive places that has seemingly thought of everything. I don't work for them, we just loved it there. Especially for me, a single mom of two, it was such an easy vacation. There were so many places to eat, and they were great. Activities. Pools. Beautiful beach. We loved it and we were excited to go back. My kids are little, so they didn't remember all I do, but they were old enough to remember the good feels of the place and we laughed and chatted on and on as we walked hand in hand to the park. About a ten-minute walk and we're there.

We saw Andrea and waved and the two of them let go of my hands to run to her. I had a quick call to take. The ceiling in my bedroom was leaking, again, and I had to speak to the guy who was going to fix it. When it rained just a little bit too hard, I'd have a little waterfall from above. I had to move my bed because I woke up soaked, having discovered the waterfall the hard way. So, the plan was that I'd hang back for a few minutes and I'd catch up with them. Andrea and I have been friends since we were little girls, and my kids love their Auntie. Whenever we go out, I tell my kids I love them, to which she says, "Auntie Andrea loves you more!" Anyway, we saw Andrea and they all headed to the other side of the park for their favorite swings, where they could swing together for an hour straight easy. And as I watched them all run together, I watched them all start to sort of, spin? Spin. They were spinning so fast that I couldn't understand what I was seeing. I couldn't hold on. And before my brain could begin to truly compute how confused I was, I was thrown to the grown. Hard. I knew it was going to bruise.

And so I hit the ground. But I didn't open my eyes yet, because I couldn't figure out much of anything. Like where I was. Like where my kids were. And why and what or who had thrown me to the ground. I tried opening my eyes, but it was so bright that I had to squint. I didn't remember it being so bright when we left the house. I wondered why I didn't bring my sunglasses. I didn't bring them. Right? I don't know. I started slowing pushing myself up from the ground, rubbing the already growing lump on my head; I had hit the ground so hard. I looked around and there was no one near me. No one had pushed me. And also, the ground was uneven. How could the ground be uneven? Where was I ? It felt like I was suddenly on the front deck of a ship in the ocean in the middle of a storm without rain, with nothing to hold onto and no-one else in sight. I couldn't hold on. I couldn't possibly stand; and the sun was so bright! Why couldn't I see the ground anymore? When did it get so bright out? What was happening?! I needed to close my eyes. Just for a quick minute.

CHAPTER THREE

The waterfall is calling

IT'S FOOD POISONING.

Y eah. Ok. I have food poisoning. That's what it must be. What can possibly come on so quickly and completely take you out like this. I was fine when we left the house, and the walk was only ten minutes. I remember the yellow daffodils, the green mint, the corner... I remember "hand train!" and waving to Andrea and my phone is ringing... Right, the waterfall is calling. No. That can't be right, but it's not ringing anymore anyway. I must have food poisoning because my whole body feels confused and I was fine ten minutes ago. Was it ten minutes ago? Why is the waterfall calling again? What's that sound? What am I hearing and how long have I been on the ground?

My kids are ok. My kids are ok. They're with Andrea. I need help. But I don't understand...I don't understand what I don't understand.

It can't be food poisoning. I gave the kids the last of the eggs, I didn't eat anything today. So, I must be contagious. We can't miss our trip. I must have a bad flu and I have to stay away from the kids, so I don't get them sick. I have ten days to feel better and I will feel better. Their dad and I weren't together anymore, and this vacation was all on me. I worked so hard to put it together, to save up vacation days, to have enough money for this. We were going on this trip. If I could just open my eyes and find my phone. But it was so bright and I felt like something was pinning me down. I was so tired. I've never felt tired like this; like a steel blanket laying on me, keeping me from moving. Why was I so hot? If I could just get someone's attention, maybe they could help me get off the ground. Maybe someone could get my kids for me. My kids are ok. They're with Andrea. Don't worry about them right now, they're ok. I just needed to open my eyes and then maybe I could understand. But I was too tired. I had to close my eyes. Just for one more minute.

CHAPTER FOUR

Ocean's 11 & Law School Daze

"Everyone needs to stay away from me". That's how it had to go. My friends helped and stayed over and took care of my kids while I slept for two days. Maybe it was three? I'd made my way into a seated position. I found my phone and I told Andrea I'd come down with something and wasn't feeling right. I asked her to give us a ride home.

I waited for them to come to me because Andrea does not ever park anywhere close to the entrance of anywhere that we're going. She has rules. She doesn't parallel park. She doesn't make left-hand turns under certain situations and I'm not going to get into the details of those rules. The point is that I waited for them.

I didn't dare walk to try to find her car because I was so damn hot! My shirt was clinging to my body, stuck there with a seemingly never-ending flow of sweat. I told everyone I was sick and needed to rest so I'd be ok for our trip, and I crawled up the stairs and got in bed.

When no one is looking, I still crawl. I've fallen down my stairs so many times. I have a very old house, that I love and that was not created with someone, who is sometimes differently-abled, in mind. I don't have a bathroom on my first floor and I'd rather crawl than fall. Again. I've figured out how to Kaiser Soze the hell out of my walking problems, but when no one's watching, I don't bother. So, I called out sick and I slept and I crawled.

Why were my feet so cold? The heating pad was too hot to touch with my hands so why didn't it warm my feet? They hurt so much from the cold, but I couldn't get them warm. But I knew I had to go back to work. A single mom without a lot of vacation days and anyway I was using so many for our trip. But how could I drive to work when I couldn't stand up without falling, even after so much sleep. If I held onto the walls as I walked, really slowly with my head down to watch my feet, then maybe I wouldn't fall. I was in-house counsel for L'Oreal USA, advertising law, and I had so much work to do. So, I got a car service to work, and they said they'd reimburse me. I was glad they knew I was worth it. I just had to fill out some paperwork and they'd reimburse me. I wish I hadn't lost that paperwork. There was just so much to do and commercials that needed review and products that needed to be launched and so much money riding on it all. I needed that job and so I held onto the walls as I walked, keeping my eyes on my feet, focusing. Focusing. I made it to my office chair where I stayed until I repeated the process and held onto the walls to get into the car service bringing me home. I just needed to make it to this vacation and I'd be ok. I was going to be ok for this vacation. I had to be ok. I wasn't sneezing or coughing, and I wasn't sick to my stomach. This wasn't any kind of sickness I'd ever experienced.

Except for that one time during my first year at Law School. That time I got so dizzy, and I couldn't get un-dizzied and the doctor said I had a bad case of vertigo. And my body was in so much pain all over and another doctor said I had fibromyalgia. And it was hard for me to focus on the words in the books, so my friend read case law to me and another doctor said I had ophthalmic migraines. And the world seemed just... so confusing. I couldn't find the right words and I couldn't figure out the order of the days and I couldn't keep straight, where I was going and what I was supposed to be doing. Everything was so suddenly and so inexplicably confusing. Until that day when it wasn't.

I went to see Oceans 11 with my sisters at that theater we'd go to near Times Square. I kept my head down as I walked and focused on my feet, trying not to fall. And we got there and we sat down and I loved that movie. Every single thing about it, I loved. It was the first time I could see clearly again. That my body wasn't screaming in pain. That I wasn't dizzy! I was coming alive again! I watched that movie and I cried because I could see it. I cried because I could understand it. I cried because I was actually able to enjoy something for the first time in what seemed like such a long, long time. I cried because whatever this awful thing was that was happening to me, had finally, just gone away. I didn't know what it was or why it left but I was so glad it was finally leaving me alone. I soaked in every single minute of that movie.

We stayed for the credits and as I watched them, I silently thanked every single person in it for being there with me. I felt good again. I was alive again. I watch that movie from time to time and I will always stay for the credits.

CHAPTER FIVE

The Deep End

Ten days, car services, feet watching, wall holding, stair crawling. Thank G-d I had packed the suitcases for all of us months ago! I felt good enough and we were off! The resort shuttle picked us up from the airport, and someone who lives in our town was on it too. What a small world. I can still feel the lobby and the warm welcome. The refreshing drinks and the cold towels. They told us they had placed the milk my kids drink in our room. This place is amazing, and I felt good. We went to our room and as always - we can unpack later because now time, is pool time. We put our suits on, and I felt so good.

Out to the pool from our ground floor room. This was our third time there and we had always stayed in the French Village. We loved the ground floor exit right to the beautiful gardens and lawns. I thought maybe next time we'd stay in the Italian village. There's a room option that includes a kid's room and video games come with their room and there are these big wooden bunk beds, OH! And a BUTLER! A butler on vacation?! A butler?! I don't have a butler in real life! The thought of having someone who could help me plan things and arrange things so I wouldn't have to figure out everything all by myself!? I thought maybe I'd have enough money for that next time. We'd do the Italian village next time, I thought.

I felt so good! I jumped in the deep end. Splash to the bottom! Cool and refreshed and I couldn't find my way up. Where were my kids? I can't breathe. I can't breathe. What's happening to me?! I made it out of the water, gasping for air, trying to see where my children were, but the sun was so bright! Where was I? I was ok when I jumped in. I felt good when I jumped in. Now clinging to the wall of the pool, I was out of the water, but I felt like I was still drowning. There had to be something so wrong with my brain. This, whatever this is, has taken over. Even when I'm feeling fine and happy and peaceful and filled with gratitude...it can advance on me and tackle me and take me down at a moment's notice. And I can't see it coming. This is dangerous. This is dangerous. And as I saw the figures of my children, blurred and warped with my confusion, I knew that this was going to be the last vacation I'd ever have with my kids. I knew I was going to die.

CHAPTER SIX

Pictures. Hands.

Deal then feel. I should trademark that. It's always been my motto. Deal now. Feel later. Handle this and don't let emotions get in the way. Handle this. Make this good for my kids. Get through this however I can. Deal now. Feel later. This is important. I had to make this vacation magical so they'd never forget it. So they'd never forget that we were happy together. So that they'd never forget, me. Deal then feel.

I took so many pictures. And videos. I watched them dance at the nightly resort-wide dance parties. My kids went up onto the stage and danced to that song by Bruno Mars about uptown funking you up and Gangnam style by PSY. I saw online that at a concert, he had a springboard under the stage and that's how he'd enter. They sort of propel him onto stage, google it, it's so cool. Look up "PSY concert stage entrance". I'll wait... Cool right?! I want to enter a stage that way some day. I don't know why I'll be on stage, and I don't know what I'll be doing but that's how I want to enter. And what's another song all the kids would dance to and sing at the top of their lungs? Ok, while you're searching on google anyway, search "my girl SNL" and watch it and then come back. All the kids loved that song. The real version, not the Kerry Washington one, but the one she did is always going to be my favorite version.

And the beaches at Beaches in Turks and Caicos. We went to the beach every day. And we went from restaurant to restaurant, dessert after dessert. The food there isn't "resort good", it's Good-Good. At every restaurant, the food is so good! We went on walks with Elmo and had breakfast with Big Bird and we counted with the Count and I drank so much water because I just couldn't quench my thirst. When I was feeling wild, I'd have a "Miami Vice" without alcohol. It was a perfect pink and white mixture of a Pina Colada and a Strawberry Daiquiri to which they'd usually add rum, but I'm allergic to rum; my allergies are odd. They offered other alcohol, but I've never been much of a drinker anyway and I was just so thirsty, everything I drank was chugged in minutes; I didn't want alcohol, I wanted something to make me not so thirsty.

And I took a picture of me holding their hands.

I wanted them to have this picture of me holding their hands on our last vacation together. I wanted them to remember this trip when I was gone. I needed them to know that in my heart, I'd always be holding their hands. I was so scared. Terrified. Not for myself, but for my babies. My kids without me. I didn't want them to be without me. But I couldn't waste this time with fear. It was only one week. Deal then feel. So, I locked my fear and sadness and terror in a tiny little box, and put the box out of sight, and we had an incredible time. Magical. And other than the crippling fear and the all over pain (that I'd also locked in that box) I felt really good.

I didn't jump in the pool again, but I walked in, holding on tightly to the walls. I realized that when I was in the water, holding onto the wall and swinging my legs, that I wasn't in any pain at all. My body loves the water and thanks me every time for entering it. If I had a pool, I'd swim every day. The sweet relief from being able to forget about the pain was exquisite. We had chocolate croissants and barefoot dinners on the beach and lazy river trips and cotton candy for miles. Our trip was perfection and I'll always thank that resort for helping me give that to my children. I felt good. And on the ride home, turning onto a street near our house, the world started violently spinning again. Oh right. Right. I remember.

My brain. My life. The pain. The confusion. My children. Their future without me. But I can't miss any more days at work.

So, I scheduled a car service for the morning.

CHAPTER SEVEN

Urgent Care and Emergency Rooms

I walked over to an urgent care the next day at lunch. The nurse moved her fingers in front of me a lot and kept asking me to touch my nose and squeeze her fingers. It was the most bizarre exam I'd ever had and it went on for some time. Touching my nose and wagging my tongue and standing on one foot at a time. I was waiting for her to tell me to put my right foot in and put my right foot out...I would have allowed a bit of Hokey Pokey. The mood was way too serious and I didn't know why. I felt like I had been thrust into a skit from <u>Kids in the Hall</u>; but I couldn't figure out the joke.

So she excused herself and came back to tell me she had called the doctor who serves that location and they both agreed I needed to go directly to an emergency room. That I needed to see a neurologist. That I couldn't drive. She was really worried about me. I could hear it in the words she spoke and I could see it in the look on her face. I asked her to give me a note stating that I couldn't drive, just in case I needed it to help me get reimbursed for the car service; the money was really adding up and I couldn't afford to keep paying so much to get to work. I just had to find that paperwork. As she handed me the note, she asked me to promise her that I'd go directly to an emergency room. I thanked her and told her I couldn't make that promise.

Who would take care of my kids if I was in an emergency room? We all know you can wait for hours and hours in an ER and you're so often overlooked even when you know what's wrong. But me? I didn't even know what was wrong with me. What would I tell them? That some nurse at an urgent care center and some doctor on the phone, who never saw me, both said I should go to an emergency room? Yeah, right. That would be a quick trip. So I went back to work, had some conference calls, spoke to my contact at ABC about a commercial I wanted them to air, checked and re-checked everything I did, got in the car to head home and made an appointment with a doctor in my town to check me out the next day.

And that doctor said I needed to go to the hospital right away. That he was worried I had an aneurism that might burst and I needed a scan immediately. And if that was all clear, he said, I needed to see a neurologist. Shit. Three people in 2 days. Neurologist. I mean, I couldn't sit up straight on the exam table because I was back on the ship's deck in the storm; I knew something was really wrong. But a neurologist? Who goes to a neurologist? But that's what would be next he said. And I went to the hospital and I got the scan and it was all clear. So the next day, I made an appointment with a neurologist.

CHAPTER EIGHT

Brain Damage and Kangaroos

So this next doctor had me lay on my side as he touched my ears a lot. And he looked in my ears and he said that he thought there were crystals in my ears or something. I don't really remember much but thinking it sounded insane and wondering if I could trust this guy. But hey, I'm the patient and he's the doctor, so maybe I have some crystals or something. He said I should go see an ENT cause I probably had an ear infection or something else; I thought that might relate to these mystical crystals. He told the intern there that whatever it was he did with my ears was often successful and again, I thought he sounded bonkers but what do I know. He's the doctor, so maybe I should just trust the guy.

I read that in Australia, lawyers are referred to as doctors. I've never been to Australia and I'm remarkably terrified of kangaroos, so I doubt I'll ever go, but I'd love to be referred to as "Doctor". I think maybe I should go back to school and get a PhD in something, cause I'm not going to med school and I want people to call me Doctor. Sometimes when I'm making dinner reservations or signing up for subscriptions to things, I choose "Dr." in the drop down menu because I am a lawyer and they don't know I'm not from Australia.

Have you ever seen a kangaroo?! Not the ones they show in cartoons because let me tell you something, they look nothing like the ones you see in cartoons.

My kids showed me a YouTube video of a kangaroo standing on his hind legs and holy hell, I locked the doors, and I turned on the house alarm. I realize that my reaction did not correlate or coincide with any realistic threat, but it made me feel better and I'd do it again. They. Are. TERRIFYING! Google them. Later. For now, focus on this book.

But wait, did you know that a group of kangaroos is called a "mob"?!? It's true! Google it. Later. I don't know if they wander the streets or live in people's back yards or what, but my kids showed me several videos, one more scary than the last and I do not ever want to come face to face with a kangaroo.

A friend of mine recently went through a bad breakup and was upset that he couldn't stop thinking about his ex, no matter what he did. Even with a lot of therapy and time passing, he couldn't stop thinking about his ex. We talked a lot about it all and I felt that wasn't really helpful enough. And I thought, words are fluff. Let's get on with the fun stuff.

So, being the good friend that I am, I hung up and then promptly sent him an email filled with pictures of kangaroos standing on their hind legs. Well, in fairness, it was a lot of emails, with a lot of pictures of kangaroos. And I followed my emails with a barrage of texts with YouTube links to kangaroos in action. I also felt it was pretty necessary for me to call him to ask him some important clarifying questions. Like, have you watched any of the videos yet. And, why haven't you watched any of the videos yet. And, if there were suddenly a mob of kangaroos in your back yard, which ones would scare you the least. And, do you think we should go to Australia to try to overcome our fears. And, if you had a pet kangaroo, what would you name it. You know, questions that I felt could really help us connect and understand each other better.

He watched all of the videos. He looked at all of the pictures. And then he texted to thank me. He felt that maybe I am a doctor, because it worked. I'm not sure I'm conveying all the details correctly, but he was impressed. Well, the conversation we had went something like:

Jessica! Enough is enough! I'M NOT THINKING ABOUT HIM ANYMORE! ALL I'M THINKING ABOUT IS ALL OF THESE TERRIFYING KANGAROOS! STOP. with the kangaroos!!! I can not keep talking about kangaroos at work! Stop!!

You're SO annoying!

It worked.

thanks doll

I love you

Jessica?

Goodness. So. many texts. It seems like you're kind of obsessed with me. Luckily, I have a solution for that. Hang on…

JESSICA!! don't. I mean it Jessica!!

Forget Jessica. I am your best friend now.

And I know he's reading this, so you're welcome. And I love you too. But that's not the point.

The point is that the neurologist doctor told me that he wanted me to get an MRI of my brain. And I told neurologist doctor that I was a single mom with two little kids. That I was all they had. That if he thought at all that there was something really wrong with me, that I needed him to be honest and tell me. He laughed and he told me I was fine, that I was worrying for nothing, that it was likely just an ear thing, and he patted me on the shoulder with a smile. I wasn't smiling. Why did he say I was "fine"? He was sending me to get an MRI of my brain. So, he wasn't sure I was fine. But that's what he told me. "You're fine". So yeah, he's the doctor. And I knew I couldn't trust this guy.

CHAPTER NINE

May 4th and 7 Letters

And for a quick lightening of the tone, I'll take this time to point out that if I hear you say "May the 4th be with you" I'll punch you in the face. Not literally, but mentally. It's all in my head, but I feel the desire behind it just the same.

You know what else will make me want to punch you in the face? If you call me "Jess". I Hate being called "Jess" or "Jessie" or anything other than the name I use when I introduce myself to people, which is only, ever, Jessica. It's 7 little letters, it really doesn't knock much time out of your day to use all of them. I've never understood the phenomenon. I say, "Hi. My name is Jessica" and people who have never ever met me before this moment, respond with, "Nice to meet you Jess!" What?!!? I mean... what?!?! Let's unpack this.

I, being me, know what my name is. I, being the person here who has known me longest, have told you what my name is. And I, the one who you just met, said that My name is JessICA. With seven letters. And then what happened next, was that You, the person here who is not Me, decided that You should choose a different name for Me? I have to say again, What?

If you call me Jess I will call you Jess in spite of whatever your name is. Unless your name is actually Jess and calling you Jess would defeat the purpose, so I will call you lampshade. I am currently looking at a lampshade and so now that will be your name. Jess, I dub thee lampshade. Everyone else, I dub thee Jess. When you get my name right, I'll try to work on yours. And if you've called me Jess before, don't worry about it, I don't remember. Just don't do it anymore. I hate being called Jess. And I am not a fan of May 4th either. 7:00 in the morning to be precise. When he showed me the screens that were filled with images of my brain damage.

CHAPTER TEN

May 3rd and Mint

I t's a weed. It grows everywhere. It attracts bees. It multiplies like crazy and, as I said, it attracts bees. And I'm allergic to bees. I have to carry an EpiPen! I got stung by a bee once and I had to go to the emergency room. It's a real thing with the bees. And also. Weedy, overgrown, multiplying all the time, mint that lives right in front of my front door... I will never cut it. I love the smell of mint.

On May 3, I went to a place in town and got a delicious falafel and their mint lemonade. And although I loved their falafels, their mint lemonade was legit the best drink I've ever tasted! It was just brilliant! The mint. Oh man, it was perfection. I remember sitting out there on Church Street at the falafel place. There's an incredible sandwich place called Dutch's in that spot now and Amir is really kind. And I can feel myself on that day, breathing in the fresh air, loving my town, loving my life, appreciating every single moment, and savoring every sip of that delicious mint lemonade.

The next day, May 4, at seven in the morning the doctor told me to look at the screen and see the dots, the marks. He told me that the marks I was looking at were scars, multiple scars. Sclerosis is a word for scars/scarring... multiple sclerosis he said. he said I had multiple sclerosis. He said it's a "Lifelong Incurable Disabling Disease". He said I have a lifelong, incurable, disabling, Disease. He said I have a lifelong. incurable. Disabling. Disease. He said I have a lifelong. Incurable. Disabling. Disease. He said Lifelong. Incurable. Disabling. Disease. I don't remember everything. But I will always remember those four words. Some things he was saying made a little sense and the rest of it, most of it, was just bat shit crazy to me. May 4th at 7 AM and my life was never the same. But May 3... May 3 is the night before.

May 3, I had no idea that I had a LifeLongIncurableDisablingDisease. On May 3, as I drank that lemonade with the perfection of that mint, I was free. I was blissfully free from those 4 words. The smell of mint is May 3. It's that lemonade and that breeze on Church Street and that blissful Blissful ignorance. The smell of mint is freedom. I don't care about the bees. I will never cut it down.

I love the smell of mint.

Chapter Eleven

Pity the Tale

M y son wrote a short story, a murder mystery, and when I read some of the lines, I knew I wanted them for this book. I asked if I could quote him and he said yes. He wrote, "One moment you're living your best life, the next you're thrust into the big world of chaos and responsibility. It all depends on which numbers you roll. I never thought I'd be here. But here I am, this is my story now." And since this is my story, I want to share with you the way I hope you'll absorb my words. To quote another literary genius, "I am not I; Pity the tale of me".

I have always loved reading, understanding and dissecting great literature. I love digging deep to get to the meaning, behind the meaning, behind the meaning. I loved the classes I took in college, I loved the teachers I had, the literature we dissected; I loved it all and I think I loved it more when I didn't understand it, because that meant a whole new way of thinking was about to emerge in my life. I loved that someone, years ago, maybe hundreds or thousands of years ago, used these words to share their innermost thoughts. And now, I get to hear them, understand them, see them. If only for a few moments, I get to bring their feelings back to life; to validate them and their experiences. I get to understand them and so often, find ways that we connect and have shared experiences. They'll never know me or anything about my world, but I know them and see them. I hope that some day, someone will read this book and feel that way about me. About my Words.

"I am not I; Pity the Tale of me". I didn't understand what those words meant, and we dissected them in class; sophomore year at UMBC. I was an English major, Sociology minor, and I loved my classes. Day after day, reading and understanding and grasping and appreciating... words. Words others have written in attempt to project their inside, out. Words used to reveal and connect people to people, one syllable at a time. I loved my college. But that's not the point.

So the words, "I am not I; Pity the tale of me", were part of a work, called "Astrophel and Stella" written by Sir Philip Sidney in the 1500s. It was a star-crossed lovers story. The man loved a woman he couldn't have and she ignored him and ignored the pain he felt in his longing for her. He noticed that when she heard a fictional story about star-crossed lovers, she cried. He was bothered that she cried about fictional people, but didn't care about him. So he said, I am not I, pity the tale of me; the story of me. Feel sorry for my story, since you won't feel sorry for me. I'll pretend I'm not real, so maybe you'll care.

Those words have never left me. My take on them is the same, but different and that's part of what I love about it. I relate to the words, even though his definition of their use isn't identical to mine. For me, it's that I would like people to hear me and understand me, and let it be just my story. I don't want anyone's pity. I'd rather look at it all as a tale I'm telling about someone who has struggled. I'd like to disconnect from it all. It's just a story, it's not real. It's how I feel about multiple sclerosis and all of the difficult times I've overcome. I step out of it and I watch it and explain it, but I don't want you to feel pity for me. It can't hurt if I'm simply the storyteller. Would I like people to be empathetic, yes. Sympathetic, yes. But feel sorry for the story only, not for me.

I ask that you please remember this. I am not I; Pity the tale of me[1].

SIR PHILIP SIDNEY'S
ASTROPHEL & STELLA
WHEREIN THE EXCELLENCE OF
SWEET POESY IS CONCLUDED
EDITED FROM THE FOLIO
OF MDXCVIII. BY
ALFRED POLLARD

LONDON
DAVID STOTT, 370, OXFORD STREET
MDCCCLXXXVIII

ASTROPHEL AND STELLA. 45

XLV.

Stella oft sees the verie face of wo
Painted in my beclowded stormie face,
But cannot skill to pitie my disgrace,
Not though thereof the cause herselfe she know :
Yet hearing late a fable, which did show
Of lovers never knowne, a grievous case,
Pitie thereof gate in her breast such place,
That, from that sea deriv'd, teares' spring did flow.
Alas, if Fancy, drawne by imag'd things
Though false, yet with free scope, more grace doth breed
Then servants' wracke, where new doubts honor brings :
Then thinke, my deare, that you in me do reed
Of lovers' ruine some sad tragedie.
I am not I ; pitie the tale of me.

1. Sidney, Philip, 1554-1586. Sir Philip Sidney's An Apology for Poetry, and, Astrophel and Stella. XLV. Pictures from books.google. com

CHAPTER TWELVE

It's all in my head

C hristina Applegate is my best friend in my head. In my head. The woman doesn't know me. I am not a crazy person. I have an actual best friend and her name is Andrea. Hi Angelina Ballerina. She's reading this right now for the 50th time because she's not only an avid reader, but she is an unbelievably loyal supporter and friend in all things. We've been best friends since we were single digit years old and we love each other. But that's not the point.

Back to Christina Applegate. She's my best friend in my head. We're around the same age and she and I have something in common that I wish we didn't. Through the social media page I created, @WeAreMontclair, where I advertise for the town and for people in the town, lately I've been talking more about multiple sclerosis and I've heard from others who have MS. As I'm writing this, there's been a long battle to get me the medicine that I'm supposed to get. Between infusion centers and health insurance and pharmacies... It's been an awful mess and it's been really really hard and taxing and stressful. I have been sharing this despite the fact that I am a very private person. And I want to share why I've chosen to share there and here, even though this is all private stuff.

There are two or three main reasons. One big reason is because of how people reacted when I shared my diagnosis. I told people how significant my privacy is to me and how I was confiding in them and didn't want them to share with anyone. And despite that, people shared with other people; people I didn't even know. This, multiple sclerosis, is the worst thing has happened in my life and I told them about it in confidence. I told them it was just for their ears. And they shared it anyway, with people who are strangers to me. Probably not in great detail. It was probably something like, "I know someone who has multiple sclerosis and blah blah blah blah blah. Oh, and so do you wanna go out to dinner tonight?" I'm sure it wasn't such a big deal. Maybe they shared a little bit more, but not much. Do you see what they did? Yes, of course, they violated my privacy. Of course, they put themselves into the category of people who are not safe spaces for me. Yes, they did those things. But it's more than that. So much more.

Because what they also did, was that they made the worst thing that's happened to me in my life, multiple sclerosis, barely a throwaway sentence or two. They made something that is monstrous to me, be something that they fit in between deciding whether or not to get soy or almond milk at Sankofa Cafe over on Orange Road. The thing that's so big to me. The monster that I trusted them to keep private with me. Those actions of theirs told me that this horrible, horrible thing for me, is nothing for them. Butter or cream cheese on your bagel. Their actions told me that what caused me pain, meant nothing to them. My pain meant nothing. Several people did this, and I'll share just two examples. Fortunately, neither of these people were of much consequence in my life. Their actions were painful nonetheless.

One of the people didn't tell me that they had told so many others and so we went to a dinner party with people who knew that I had multiple sclerosis. But I didn't know that they knew. My little sister didn't know yet. But these people all knew. And so people I didn't know came up to me with sad eyes and took my hands in their hands and looked at me and said... "Are you OK!??". I had no idea what they were talking about. But even if I had immediately figured it out, it was all a jumbled mess in my own mind. I didn't know how to answer the question of if I'm OK. Of course I'm not, but how do you answer that to someone who doesn't have multiple sclerosis? They don't understand. They can't. And I was barely holding it together at that time. I was a wreck emotionally. I was terrified and scared and worried for myself and for my children... And that person who I had trusted with this information, had shared with these people who now felt it was their right, because they were trying to be "nice", to talk about the disease I have. At a dinner party. With people I didn't know. It was awful. They all knew each other and I didn't know any of them. I was totally on my own. And it was now on me to be pleasant and to figure out how to end this conversation about my private health issues. A conversation I certainly didn't want to have with these people; at this place. And now I had to maneuver my way out of it. While I was being told by the mistake who brought me there, that I just didn't understand that everyone was trying to be "nice"; it wasn't all intrusive or insensitive or inappropriate or unkind. "Nice". And I wasn't being grateful for their concern. I was being too sensitive. That's how the mistake treated me.

It was now on me to manage everyone else's feelings about my no-longer-private misery. No apology was ever given. Frankly, the damage was done. If I had been of clearer mind at the time, I would have annulled that mistake from my life that night; before that night. The thankfully brief connection, was an unfortunate and sad side effect of having suddenly become an incurable, disabled person. I had met them years earlier and instantly, strongly disliked them. It wasn't until I was terribly sick, weakened and scared that I allowed them into my world at all.

Another person who I trusted with this information, needed to tell me about a person they connected with online, who is an herbalist. An herbalist who they said had cured someone of multiple sclerosis, or had claimed to have gotten someone's mailman's cousin's brother, off of their multiple sclerosis medication. I don't remember the exact details of their amazing feats, because it was all nonsense not worth committing to memory. It was nonsense and it was unbelievably reckless and careless and stupid to say. But this person who

I trusted with this information, who had promised to keep it private, had not only discussed it with somebody else, but then had the chutzpah to contact me to give me this "herbalist's" recommendations on my healthcare. Jesus Christ.

And then, as so many people do, they both got offended. And they felt it was on me to defend my position of not wanting to hear, much less follow, the "guidance" provided in their trainwreck of misinformation. I didn't want to know their "justification" for breaking my trust in them. Their egos were bruised because I wasn't excited about their betrayal, their back-stabbing-advice.

Advice that wasn't asked for, wasn't wanted, was repetitive and reckless and left me to think of all of the times I wanted to and tried to believe. It made me think of people I knew who did believe the nonsense and now can't walk. Made me think of how lonely it is to have a disease that no one understands and so many insist on speaking about anyway. Made me think of the times I was let down by the latest fad "solution" and then had to be the one to comfort the person providing the service, because of course it didn't work. And now they felt bad or sad or mad... and now I had to manage their feelings even though I'm the one with the disease... all of that and more is what goes through our minds when unasked for and uninformed suggestions are made about this disease. It not only doesn't help. It hurts. It causes heartache. It causes emotional pain. Pain like when lil dinner party boy and the herbalist kiddo shared my private health issues with strangers.

What awful things to do to someone who has trusted you. With the worst thing that's ever happened to them. If you meet anyone with multiple sclerosis, please, don't be guilty of any of this.

So that's the first thing that made me start talking openly about having multiple sclerosis. And there's a second reason but now I know what chapter has to come next.

CHAPTER THIRTEEN

Bad Decisions

I made so many of them. Financial bad decisions. Relationship bad decisions. Work bad decisions. Donation bad decisions. So many, so many, I made so many bad decisions, and I felt so angry at myself for every one of them. Disgusted with myself. Filled with regret and shame for my stupid decisions that I never would have made before now. Why was I being so stupid? Weak? Why was I allowing awful people, awful treatment, why was I allowing this in my life. I was disgusted with myself for my bad decisions. I was filled with sorrow in a tunnel that had no light at the end.

When I was diagnosed with MS, I felt like I had been plunged into darkness, and looking back, it seems that I would cling to anyone who happened to come by with anything that even resembled a flashlight. But when I was able to see even a sliver of light on my own, I quickly saw that those flashlights were garbage. Not only did they fail to bring any light in, but they were plunging me deeper into the dark.

People took advantage of me. Of my kindness. Of my patience. Of my money. I am out so much money that I'll never see again because of those damned crappy pseudo flashlights. To this day, I am still paying financially for my ill-informed, misguided, misplaced trust.

I spoke to a therapist who summed it up for me in a way I hadn't thought of and now think of for myself and for so many others too. When something crazy happens to you and you react, the thing is the crazy. Not you. That thing is bad. Not. You.

If a bomb explodes in the middle of a busy street with people everywhere, tell me which reaction is wrong. Is it the guy who stands there in shock watching the explosion? Is it the guy who runs screaming and crying? Is it the guy who falls to his knees and records a video to say goodbye to his mother? Is it the guy who calls his ex to let them know he still loves them. Is it the guy who shakes his head and laughs as he walks away to his lunch appointment ... which one is wrong. Which one? None of them. They're all right. They're all human beings organically reacting to something shocking. Something awful. Unexpected. Destructive. That thing. That bomb- THAT is the wrong thing. And every single person's reaction... is right.

Never shame yourself for reacting to a bomb explosion. Applaud yourself for being alive. Applaud yourself for trying. Applaud yourself because in that moment, and in these moments as you're surviving the aftermath of the bomb, you are a human being who is trying to live. And know that if you make some bad decisions, when the time is right, you will realize it and you will do the best you can to move on. Know that you must must Must forgive yourself for not knowing what you didn't know. Forgive yourself. Throw out those crappy flashlights. And move on.

CHAPTER FOURTEEN

And back to the second reason I started sharing

So my town had a festival. My town is known for festivals. My town is incredible. So I went to meet up with a lot of business owners that I support on social media, and of course to enjoy it and to have a really nice day. I went alone, which I decided to do, because I wanted to take a lot of pictures and videos and maybe interview some people and catch up with some friends. So it was best that I was on my own doing this. It's my hobby but I was seeing it as if that day was a day for me to do my "job" of supporting my town. I was excited about how well businesses were going to do and how much fun I knew people would have.

There were so many people there, some I had and some I hadn't met in person yet. There were thousands and thousands of people at this festival. It was an arts and crafts fair type, where they closed down a main road and there were bunches of vendors up and down. And all of the stores and restaurants on that street participate too. It's a great thing. One of my social media followers works with the group that puts the event together, and she keeps me updated about things that are happening. She let me know when it had to get canceled this year because of rain. Boo. I mean not rain, but you know what I mean... It's rescheduled. But that's not the point. The point is that I went. I drove there. I walked around and had a wonderful time. It wasn't very hot and I wasn't tired. I drink water all of the time, so I was very well hydrated as usual. I felt great.

And maybe about an hour and a half in, after taking lots of pictures and videos, suddenly, I had no idea where I was. I had absolutely no idea where I was. I didn't know how I got there. I couldn't figure out what was happening. It was like there were just these swarms of people surrounding me and I was so confused and so scared. This can happen with multiple sclerosis, as some of you know. I think my brain just got overloaded and I needed to regroup? Take a minute? Maybe with all of the people, with all the walking, with all of the stimulation to my brain? I don't know, but it's the most sense I can make of it. That, thankfully, doesn't happen to me anymore so if you're reading this, don't try to kidnap me and pull an "Overboard" with Goldie Hawn. Seriously. Kidnapping and quicksand were my biggest fears when I was a kid. But that's not the point.

So because it had happened before, I decided to stand where I was, lean on this brick wall of a building, and just be confused. I didn't try to figure anything out. I didn't try to understand a thing. I just stopped thinking. I just didn't think. Ladies, do you know that men can actually do that? They can literally just stop thinking. How beautiful that must be. But that's not the point.

I stood and I watched the world continue to go by. I was too dizzy to close my eyes, so I kept still, breathed and waited to understand whatever it was that I wasn't understanding. And eventually, I figured out where I was and what was going on. I couldn't figure out where my car was and was too unstable to drive anyway. I didn't call anyone, cause what would I say? How could I explain? So I walked home. And I cried the whole way.

And later, I went back with my friend and got my car. I could've driven by then, but I kind of wanted a friend. And then later I thought, oh my Lord... I was in a crowd of thousands of people and I was completely alone. I was in a crowd of thousands of people and nobody could see what was happening to me. I was invisible and alone. But I had just met up with, talked with, taken pictures with 50? 30? 100? people and all of them know me and like me. And all of them would help me in a heartbeat. And none of them knew. So I was alone. And I decided, enough was enough. As hard as it was to talk about it and as hard as it was to share it. I didn't want to be invisible in a crowd of thousands. That confusion and that fear didn't have to be that way. The isolation that comes with M.S. is bad enough.

And there truly is a unique sense of isolation and loneliness that comes with multiple sclerosis. It's like being given a life sentence of solitary confinement when you haven't committed a crime. Just scooped up one day and thrown into isolation. And nobody knows why. And no one knows how to get you out. And no one knows what happens to people in isolation, and no one knows what it looks like in there, so you quickly become invisible. Out of sight, out of mind. I didn't want to be invisible. I don't want to be invisible. So that's why I started telling people and also...

CHAPTER FIFTEEN

I don't remember

There was a third reason and I don't remember it. And it's big. And that's a fun part of multiple sclerosis too. If you know, you know. I'm thinking about the forgetfulness but also the balance and the falling down and the surgeries after the bad falls and the years, Years, I was covered in bruises, because I fell all of the time. And all of the dropped food, and the meals I burned and the forgotten appointments, and the inability to think of that word when you know what that word is and it's swimming around your head, but you can't grab it, but it's right there, but you can't grab it. And the look of the doctors faces when they don't know what to do with you, and the hopeful look on your friends faces when they ask you if the infusion medication you're getting is "healing you" or making you "better". It's lonely. When nobody speaks your language. It's lonely. When you don't know where you are. It's lonely. It's lonely in isolation. If I remember what I was going to say, I'll add it another time.

Chapter Sixteen

Watch out for the Snake Oil

So I wasn't sure about telling people about my diagnosis, and a large part of why I still hesitate, is because I got so many nonsensical, idiotic recommendations for herbs and chakra balancing and frog venom injections and on and on. I'm not knocking all of that stuff but come on y'all. Stop. There are so many people who got their degrees in healthcare on the Internet. Hey, I'm an ordained minister. I could perform your marriage ceremony. You know how I got that ordination? I went online and clicked on a box and it said "Congratulations! You are now an ordained minister!" And it was free. Anyone could do it. You can pay some money to get the paperwork to find out some more stuff about the legalities or how to file paperwork and stuff and so I guess that's how they make money, but... I don't want any part of anyone who takes bullshit, that they know is bullshit, that they know is not healthcare, and bullshits people because it's a money making business for them. We all need money and I'm not knocking anybody who tries to make a business out of what they feel they can do. I'm not against anybody, who learns something, even on the Internet, that teaches them to help people.

However, I am against the people whose lives are miserable, first of all, and then tell you that they can fix yours. But more than that, I'm against the people who know damn well that they're snake oil salesman. They know damn well that they aren't really doing anything. I have friends who I had to stop being friends with because they literally said to me, "I don't know what I'm doing". But they would still sell their services and promise to "heal". Have you noticed that everyone seems to be qualified now to be a healer? A life coach? A chakra balancer? A reiki master? Amazing that the world isn't in better shape with so many healers out there. Snake oil. You have to watch out for the snake oil.

When you are diagnosed with a lifelong incurable disabling disease it is fucking devastating. It is devastating in a way that you don't know unless you have been through it. And you can be really desperate. A lot of us are really desperate. Especially in the beginning. And when someone who knows they can't actually do a damn thing to help, chooses to take the money of someone who is desperate ... That's fucking horrible. That's fucking horrible. I'll balance my own chakras, thank you. Hold the Goji berries.

Chapter Seventeen

Coal Mines

See the thing is that if you work in a coal mine, you know what it feels like in a coal mine. You know the temperature of a coal mine as you descend. You know the air quality in the coal mine. You know of the smell and of the cold and of the specific darkness and dampness. You know the feeling in detail, of descending into that darkness; that eye adjustment, that temperature change, that cold, damp darkness.

You can tell your significant other about the coldness and of the smell and of the feeling and of the descent. You can explain to your doctor about how the work affects your body and your health. You can tell your friends about the medicine you have to take to try to help with your lungs and other physical results of working in a coal mine. You can cry to your best friend, you can tell your children, you can write it online. And even if every single person who has absorbed your words, cares about you and is 100% on your side... None of them will ever know what it feels like to be you, descending into the coal mine. None of them have the right to tell you how to feel about your body or your mind. You descend into the mine alone; every day and every night. And unless they descended with you. Exactly and literally with you every single time... they cannot possibly know how it feels. They cannot possibly know. It's solitary confinement. A Life Sentence.

CHAPTER EIGHTEEN

I am grateful and we've never met

S o as I said, Christina Applegate is my best friend in my head. I've appreciated everything I have read that she has allegedly said about the thing that we have in common; you know Voldemort. It feels like they're my words coming out of my mouth. And it stops me in my tracks because for the most part, nobody else speaks my language anymore. And we're such best friends in my head, it's like we're like she was with Judy in that TV show she had which was so Flippin amazing! I think it was called "Dead to Me", but I'll check before I commit to that. It was so good! Wait a minute, is that the movie with Kenneth Branagh maybe? Oh my gosh, did you see that movie? Dead to me? Dead again? I was in undergrad when that came out and I saw it with a bunch of friends. One of my friends, literally had such a jump scare that he landed in my lap. Like a literal jump scare. That movie is so good. Oh my gosh, and it will make you cry too. Just preparing you. But it's so good! Do not let that deter you. But that's not the point.

When I started writing this book, I almost started with the actress Terri Garr. She made a statement in an interview about "Voldemort", and it stopped me in my tracks. I watched it very soon after I had been diagnosed and my jaw dropped. Someone said to her "what's multiple sclerosis like" or "what's it like having multiple sclerosis" and she looked at them and she said "it sucks". Fuck, yes. Fuck. Yes. YESSSSSS!! IT SUCKS!! And she called it like it was, when everybody else was saying "lighten up" and "it could be worse" and "it will be better" and "don't worry" or "do worry" or "get some sleep" or "eat some dark green leafy vegetables" or "meditate", " do yoga" or whatever the fuck people are saying all the fucking time, avoiding the fact that it <u>fucking</u> <u>sucks</u>. It Sucks ! It's awful! It's horrible! It's a fucking monster that has invaded my life and my body and I can't get rid of it! Nobody knows why it intruded upon my life! Nobody knows why it invaded my body! And fucking nobody knows how to make it leave. Because as of now, no matter what your herbalist tells you, there's no way to make it leave yet.

And I've heard the things that my best friend in my head has said, and I hear myself. And when I see the look on her face, I see myself. And I want to give my best friend in my head a hug because not only would it be hugging somebody else who is going through something when I know exactly how they're trudging through. But also because it would be like hugging myself. Feeling like somebody's hugging me too, who sees me too.

And through my social media page, through my talking about having multiple sclerosis, although I've heard some unbelievable nonsense... Multiple people who also have multiple sclerosis have reached out to me. My words resonate with them. They have reached out to me and said that they've seen me in my videos when I talk about multiple sclerosis and they identify with it. And when some of them speak, it's like my best friend in my head speaking, it's like I'm speaking. We speak each other's language. And I'm thankful for that. My in person friends, my online friends, my Bestie Andrea And Christina Applegate... My best friend in my head. For all of them, I am grateful.

CHAPTER NINETEEN

I just remembered

D ammit. I had a really good idea but my doctor's office called and I lost my flow and I'm frustrated. They told me that I don't need to worry that this Saturday will be a month late for me to get the infusion; a month late because of all the mixups and mis-management of my care by the infusion center, the health insurance, the pharmacy...They told me that the infusion center was supposed to call me this morning to schedule my infusion. Of course they haven't. They told me not to worry because medically I'm OK. I told them that that's only a portion of it. But I don't think they understand. And that, I don't understand.

I was told that I had to have this medicine in two weeks and now they're saying that it's OK if I don't have it for four weeks or for 4 months... My doctor told me that it was OK if I don't have it for up to four months. But the medicine is scheduled precisely at a certain time. The first dose and then two weeks later the second dose. One of my friends who I met through my social media page is on the same medicine. She got it. And then two weeks later, she got the second dose. And she was done. That's the way it was scheduled. I would think for a reason?

And this medicine. I'm terrified that 20 years from now, 30 years from now, we're going to find out that this infusion medication that I'm fighting so hard to get, causes cancer. I'm terrified about taking this. I feel like I'm on the edge of a cliff and someone's going push me off if I don't jump. Those are my options. I don't know how far the ground is. I don't know if there is ground. I don't know if there's water. I don't know if there's lava. Did you ever play that game "floor is lava"? I still play that with my kids in hotels. My kids are my favorite people in the entire world. How lucky am I that I happen to live with my favorite people? They're magnificent and I love doing anything with them. We always play floor is lava in the hallways of hotels, but it's really good if you play it in the hotel room and there are multiple beds because the beds aren't lava but all of the floor space is and you have to jump on pillows to get out of the room. But that's not the point.

The point is that I'm jumping off a cliff and I don't know what I'm jumping into and I'm only jumping because otherwise someone will push me. Those are the choices of someone getting infusion medication with multiple sclerosis. Jump or be pushed. I don't want either and I don't have a choice. And I'm fighting so hard to get this thing that I don't want. That I'm scared of. That I think is going to hurt me in the long run and that I don't even know will help me now. But I've psyched myself out to go to these appointments. To get these infusions. I put a lot of mental energy and work and emotional care for myself and for my children to get myself to and from these infusions.

And week after week 30 minutes before I was supposed to go, I got a phone call saying- Oopsie we don't have it for XYZ reason. I appreciate the doctors office telling me that it's not medically necessary that I get it when the medicine says that it's medically necessary to get it. When everybody else taking this medicine gets it. I appreciate them telling me that I don't need to worry about my health. Which makes no sense to me, but I appreciate them telling it to me and still... The emotional and mental stress is immense. The logistics alone. It's not just "frustrating" or "annoying". Frustrating is when your phone didn't fully charge. Annoying is when the printer is jammed. This isn't that. And I do not understand how anybody can fail to understand. I do not understand.

People who have chosen to work in a field with an incurable disabling disease that can be worsened by stress. I don't understand what they don't understand.

And I just remembered what I wanted to say in this chapter. That seems like a good title for this chapter. So I'm going to name this and move on to the next.

CHAPTER TWENTY

Triage

I've met some caring, helpful people over the past six years. And also, I've met others. And I wonder if some who have chosen to work with people who have MS, simply become desensitized to it. Because everyone has it, there's nothing special or unique about it so everyone is treated with the same casual/dismissive attitude. And the ones who look fine and seem fine, are really just annoying to the people in the field. Because of course, there are people with MS who are outwardly, obviously, physically suffering and struggling. So if everyone has the same thing, and some are far worse, then those are the ones who are worth the attention and time. The ones who aren't so outwardly obviously bad, should quiet down and do what they're told and not bother the healthcare professionals, who are busy focusing on people who really need it. And if that's not you, then your focus should be on gratitude that it's not you. Why are you complaining. Everyone we see has it. You're not that bad. You're asking too many questions. Emotional. Just take your medicine and get the MRIs and get the bloodwork and "don't worry" and smile and nod and thank everyone for smiling at you. And don't complain. Everyone has it. I wonder sometimes if they're just numb. Or not properly trained. Or if this is just a job and they don't really care. And I wish I had never met any of them. They chose to be involved with this disease. I have no damn choice. I don't want to meet any of them. I don't want to meet anymore of these people.

Without eye contact or even turning to face you, rate your pain from 1-10. And now try to figure out what the worst of the stuff is that you're experiencing. Cause there's so much and you barely have their attention as it is. And why bother. It's just another disinterested clerk. You'll just have to repeat it all when the doctor comes in anyway.

Triage your life. As you do every day because you can't, no one can, be on the front line of every battle. No one can fight in every war. Figure out which doctor to see for which problem. Figure out how to get there and how to schedule your kids around your appointments. Figure out how much money it will cost out of pocket to see this doctor. Find out if it will be one visit or many, because scheduling something that requires you to be there many times, is simply not realistic anymore. Figure out which doctor might help, so maybe you don't have to mention that one problem here. They're not paying attention. They can't help you anyway. And you'll have to say it all again, when the doctor appears.

So much goes into every single appointment for the MS patient but for the people who see this every day? Ho hum. Data entry. No eye contact. No humanity. Wait for the doctor and repeat it all again. Then make that appointment for next time, so you can do it in 6 months. Again and again. Hamster wheel. Cog in a machine. Carbon copy of everyone else. And your pain, and your fear and your sadness, your privacy, are just words to be scratched down in a chart. That anyone there can read or not read at-will. People you don't know, all get to read it all. You don't even know their names but they can access your life. Reduced to this, every 6 months. Just smile and wait for the doctor.

Not all of them are this way. But one is too many and I've met far more than one and I wish I'd never met any of them. I wish I had no reason to know these people. I don't want to know these people and I sure as hell don't want these people to have access to my private information. But what's private anymore when you have this disease. Stranger after stranger. Private personal questions from disinterested stranger after stranger. Thank you, next.

So sayeth Ariana Grande. So sayeth I.

CHAPTER TWENTY-ONE

Dr. I'm Screwed

I was in so much pain. My left foot was in so much pain. I've never broken a limb, and this, to me, felt like a broken foot. But I hadn't done anything to it. I hadn't done any out of the ordinary exercises or jumping of any kind. I hadn't dropped anything on it, I hadn't been in an accident. But my foot was in so much pain. You're always asked how much pain you're in on a scale from to scale 1 to 10. And this was about level 7-8 pain. It was bad and I couldn't figure it out. I was crying and limping and added to the hip pain and hand pain, all together, I just couldn't function properly, so I made an appointment with a doctor. He poked and probed, which was incredibly painful, but led him to the conclusion, that my foot was not broken. As he started to flip through my paperwork, he came across something that gave him that look. "The look" that multiple sclerosis patients learn to know. The look that says, "oh, you have multiple sclerosis... I can't help you." The look that says, " I don't know what's really wrong with you. Nobody does. You're kind of screwed." The look that says, "I've gotta get you out of here because there are patients here who I can help, and I need to spend my time and energy on them." And the look always accompanied by glances at their watch or the clock on the wall, and that's a combination of the following three:

1) Here's a prescription for physical therapy. I have no clue what's wrong or how it could help, but it's off my plate now and I can move on and you can leave.

2) Here's a prescription for painkillers. They're very strong and addictive and you'll be pretty comatose and non functional if you take them. But it will get you out of this pain. And it will get you out of my office. I can move on and you can leave.

3) I can't see anything I can diagnose. I can't see anything physically wrong with you. So even though you seem intelligent and rational and seem like you have it together, you must actually be an emotional wreck. You must actually be really off balance emotionally. There must not be any pain. It's all in your head, so I'm going to tell you that you need see a therapist. Maybe when you get your emotions in check, your foot won't hurt anymore. You're doing this to yourself. It's your fault. Go talk it out with someone, I need to move on. You can leave.

Time passed and I went to see another doctor. The pain was now worse. 10 out of 10. And then the exam and the pain and the conclusion that it wasn't broken. And then the big MS reveal and the glazed confusion set in. And I asked if he could just take and X-ray or some kind of a scan, because something was very wrong. Because I didn't want to pop more Oxy. Because I'm not making this up. It's not because I'm sad. It's because I'm in awful, pain, would you take some sort of a test or scan?

Nope.

MS Glaze.

Drugs. Physical Therapy. Therapy Therapy. Goodbye.

So I went to a third doctor. 12 out of 10 pain. And in the spot on the paperwork for illnesses or disease...I left it blank. I needed this doctor to look at me as if I did Not have multiple sclerosis. As if I was someone worth the time to diagnose. As if I was someone whose problem might be fixed. As if I was someone in so much pain and not able to walk and on my third doctor and I needed someone to help me. So I left it blank. And he ordered a scan. And because I could access the portal and I read the report, I knew that I had a hairline fracture. That had likely gotten worse over the months it took me to get to this point. I was so relieved when I saw the doctor was calling, because now we knew what was wrong and we could make a plan. But it wasn't the doctor. It was his receptionist. It was his receptionist telling me that the doctor told her to call me to tell me that he would not be taking me on as a patient. Because he'd learned that I have multiple sclerosis; I suppose any prescribing doctor gets to rifle through a patients medical history, even without express permission given by the patient? I don't know. So he found out that I had multiple sclerosis. Since I had not shared it with him, he told this woman to call and scold me for being dishonest with them. No discussion of the fracture I now knew I had. No discussion of my treatment options. Just admonishment for being a naughty little liar and goodbye.

So I googled it. And I ordered a boot for my foot from Amazon. And I used ice packs. And I took some advil. And I rested my foot whenever I could. And I realized that this was now my reality. That when I'm in pain, doctors won't try to help me if I tell them I have MS.
But if I don't tell them I have MS, and it is within their power to help me, they won't help me.
Because I didn't tell them I have MS.

If I tell them, they won't help me.
If I don't tell them, they won't help me.
Oh my G-d.

I'm screwed.

CHAPTER TWENTY-TWO

Spoiler Alert. No one speaks your language

I t really is like you're walking down the street one day and someone grabs you and throws you into a cell. With a Huge. Indescribable. Monster. It's like nothing you've ever seen or heard of before and it's taking up most of the space in this cell. And no one can tell you why you're in it and where this monster came from and why it's there with you. They don't know how to get you out.

And you don't understand where you are; you can't possibly. You don't understand what's happening. Every day is a different kind of new thing that ranges from strange to absolutely miserable to 12 out of 10 pain. I saw a doctor who told me that multiple sclerosis isn't a painful disease. I had a physical therapist tell me that I got multiple sclerosis because I needed to learn lessons about life. I had another "healthcare" person tell me that I'll learn to appreciate my children now that I have MS. None of these people knew me before our first (and last) meetings and none of them had multiple sclerosis. Lovely. Lovely. And so helpful.

Suddenly, you're in this cell and your entire existence is now strange or bad or painful or some combination of all of them, but in a different way. You have no idea what's happening and you're trying so hard to figure it out because you still have the rest of your life to manage. And this monster is obstructing your view! It's right there in plain sight and yet somehow, you can't see it. No one can! You can't even really describe it. But, it can touch you. It can hurt you. And it can do that all while remaining invisible. All while taking the air and the space in this tiny cell you're now inhabiting against your will. And you have a house, you have a family, you have children, you have a job, you have bills, you have other worries, and stresses, you have relationships. But you're in this fucking cell! You've been thrown into this fucking cell. With this fucking monster!

And what's even worse than that, is that nobody else speaks your language. You're desperately trying to grasp for words, literally or figuratively, but you can't. You don't know what this monster wants from you. You don't know how far this monster is going to go to hurt you. You don't know if all of the pain and the shaking and the confusion and the ... you don't even know for sure if the monster is causing all of it. But there's no way to know, because the monster is invisible. And no one speaks your language. And you're trapped in this cell, that seems to be getting smaller every day.

And so you do the absolute best you can to get the right words out to explain, to get people to understand. You try to move in a way that won't make the monster try to hurt you; even though you're just making it up as you go. You try to move in a way that won't make the monster wipe your memory or gaslight you or exhaust you or make you so hot or so painfully cold. And you're making it up as you go. All alone in this ever shrinking cell. And any time you're able to put the words together to try to get someone to hear you, you're reminded that nobody speaks your fucking language anymore.

It's so lonely.

Nobody else knows what it's like to live in that cell with that monster.

So I'm thankful for my best friend in my head. Cause in my head, we hang out and we're besties like she was with Judy on " Dead to Me" and we go swimming at night and we smoke pot (or eat some gummies from Blue Oak) and laugh and cry and drink some wine. But in our version, nobody's murdered like in the show. Dammit. Spoiler alert. You're supposed to say that first. Maybe I'll add spoiler alert to the title of this chapter. You gotta watch that show. That series. Oh my gosh... How about this...

How about we have a viewing party. If you get me and if you understand me, let's have a viewing party. But do you have a pool? Because I don't. When I'm in water is the only time I feel no pain. And someday in my future dream life I'm gonna have a pool. I want an indoor pool and an outdoor pool, I said. You hear me Beyoncé & JAY-Z? I need an indoor and an outdoor pool. Have you seen their house?! Google it. If I had a house like that, I'd swim any time of year. Actually, I'm not sure they have an indoor pool, but I bet they do. If I could get in the pool every day, I could have a little bit of time when I'm not in pain. Every day, I could have moments when my foot and my leg don't drive me crazy with that pop-rocks sensation. I would like to have a time out from all of it. But that's not the point.

The point is that if you have a pool, and if you're cool, I made a rhyme. I ate a lime. No I didn't. This is dumb. If you have a pool and you're a normal person, let's have a viewing party of the show with my best friend in my head, Applegate. Let's binge watch a few episodes and let's drink some good wine. I don't really know anything about wine, so not expensive wine, because I don't know that I could taste the difference between... I like that wine ...what's that Snoop Dogg wine? You know what I mean? It says something about... I can't remember but that's my price point in red wine. I only like red wine. I don't like white wine. I don't ever drink more than one glass anyway. I usually don't like champagne either, but I tasted some champagne I liked at an event the local museum had. Oh! You know who has a champagne line? Kool & The Gang! Le Kool Grand Cru; I haven't tried it yet but I love the name. I always wanted to be in one of their videos. I used to wish my name was Joanna so that I could be in the music video and the song would be about me. I think I want to make a music video with that song in the background with friends of mine dancing around. Diane Carroll said something like, "if they don't invite you to the party, throw your own". They didn't know me so it's OK they didn't invite me to be in their music video; but the point is that they didn't. So why don't I make my own! I am brilliant. I don't even remember the point of this... I'm just going to end it. But what's the point of this... actually I'll have to continue later.

I have to go because someone is coming by because my daughter is going to be babysitting for their kid. I want to give them a heads up about me and multiple sclerosis and also about the fact that my children's father passed away soon after I was diagnosed with MS. I collapsed and was diagnosed with a lifelong, disabling, incurable, disease. He collapsed a few months later and died instantly.

That year. For my children. All of this and the affects on my children...

I don't usually discuss any of this, for so many reasons; I've always been a very private person. I don't share with most people. But my daughter will be babysitting their kid who is little. And I feel that it could be upsetting if their kid says something about- where is your dad -or -why is your mom in the hospital- or something like that, it could be sad and uncomfortable for my kid. And it could be sad and scary for theirs. I just want to give them a heads up so that they can get ahead of it and manage it however they want to with their kid. So, I want to tell them. And also, my house is a mess. So, I have to go and randomly spray Lysol. Or maybe some Endust. Oh! And I should put out a roll of paper towels, like, "phew you just saved me from cleaning!" Yeah. I'm not cleaning at all. Cause that's how I'm gonna roll today. This is tricky stuff. OK I'll write more later.

CHAPTER TWENTY-THREE

Charlie and the Story Salon

T he visit went fine. The family is kind. I'm glad I filled them in. I still haven't cleaned. And a fabulous actress in my town hosts a "Story Salon". She has people and artists and musicians come and tell their personal stories. She gives the theme and they tell the story and she asked me to speak. What I wrote below is what I said at the story salon; it's written this way because these are the notes I read from that night. Some parts of it will be repetitive, but I want you to read it anyway. The theme was "Grow for me".

And when all of the stories were told, a man named Charlie , who I had never met before, came up to me and said that he couldn't believe that I'd ever been made to feel invisible. He said that my presence and my goodness filled the room. He said that he was sorry that anyone ever made me feel invisible and he gave me a hug. A lot of people that night came up to me because they heard me. They didn't pity me. They felt pity for the tale of me. They wanted me to know that they were sorry that I felt that invisible. What a nice thing to do. For a stranger... What a nice thing to do. Please read this. After all, this chapter has already been written. Please see me.

I grew up in Montclair riding bikes, climbing trees, playing in Tony's Brook. Back in the 1900s before cell phones and playdates-when parents told their kids-go outside! play! We played A LOT in Tony's Brook. At the way back of our property was a big fence and on the other side was the brook-where we played for hours and hours and it was wonderful, my childhood here. Like a movie. AND One of those days I got lost and it was scary So. My mom and I got bunches of yellow daffodils and planted them at the base of our property. There were a lot of trees and not a lot of sun down there, not the best place to plant- but we planted anyway and my mother said - when you see the yellow daffodils you'll know that you're home. brilliant. I never got lost again.

And what I loved about those daffodils, in addition to the fact that they were there, growing for me, to let me know that I was home ...was that they were planted. rooted. where we put them, But! they were not immobile. They would lean into that little bit of sun. They were strong, resilient, smart, and adaptable in conditions that weren't so great for them. I absolutely loved that! I thought it was magical that they knew they needed to survive & grow for me & to do that, they needed to lean into the sun. And all my life, whenever I moved, undergrad, law school, I'd buy myself a few yellow daffodils. When I bought my house, I planted a couple right in front And!...

On a March 31, not so long ago, my kids and I headed to the park nearby, past our daffodils, a ten minute walk. We talked about our upcoming trip to Turks & Caicos, only 10 days away! laughing and joking & as soon as we got there, the kids ran off to the swings. And the world, for me, started spinning. Violently spinning. So violently that I was thrown down to the ground. I couldn't figure out what was going on ...because I was GREAT ten minutes ago! So ...I figured I had some sort of flu & I had to keep away from the kids so I wouldn't get them sick too! SO! Ten days later! I was ok enough! and we went on vacation!

We got to the hotel, we threw our bathing suits on, we went to the pool, I jumped in the water and realized I couldn't find my way up. I was so dizzy and so confused & I knew then that there was something very wrong with brain. I believed I was going to die and that this was going to be the last vacation I'd ever have with my kids SO! this had to be the best vacation we ever had.

I took so many pictures. I took this picture of my hand holding my kids' hands. I wanted them to have this picture of me holding their hands on our last vacation together. I put all of my worries & fears in a box, I set them aside and We had a Fantastictime AND! on our way home from this magical vacation, turning onto Bloomfield Ave, the world started violently spinning again just like it had in the park on March 31 .

So...doctors, exams, hospitals, scans and on May 4 at 7...May the 4th be with you...I hate May 4th at 7 in the morning the doctor showed me these pictures -of my brain and my spine and he said the gray parts were normal and healthy but the white spots. That were everywhere. They were scars. damage. spine damage. Brain. damage. they were scars. He said. the Plural... is sclerosis. He said. I had multiple. sclerosis on my brain on my spine. He said. I had multiple sclerosis.he said it's a lifelong, incurable, disabling, disease. He said.

multiple sclerosis messes with everybody differently at different times , and for me at that time, I was so dizzy that I couldn't stand up without falling to the ground- I was covered in bruises. I had to learn how to walk again- twice since then-I've had to learn how to walk again. I couldn't climb stairs because I couldn't get my balance, I fell down flights and ended up in ambulances. In surgeries. I couldn't navigate when I was driving anywhere because my brain would forget things-right in front of Grove Pharmacy on Grove street, I had no idea where I was. I couldn't cook in the oven- I'd forget that I was cooking and I'd burn the dinner. and I couldn't cook on the stove because my hand would start shaking and I'd drop everything that I cooked on the floor and I couldn't hold my children's hands when we crossed the street because i couldn't risk bringing them down.

I'd become this person who couldn't.

I was OK on March 31 when we left our house, we walked past the daffodils and now I was this person who couldn't and who would my children remember? the person who rode bikes & climbed trees & jumped into the pool with them on vacations. Or the Person. who couldn't. who couldn't even hold their hands when we crossed the street. AND I was so sad and so angry and sooo frustrated -so frustrated with all the well meaning people with all of the WORDS, you know...

...the person who's got a cousin who's an herbalist who cured their mailman's brother of MS AND when was the last time you had your chakras balanced AND have you heard about the frog in the Amazon who excretes this venom that can fix... you know! Anger isn't good for anyone, you really shouldn't... Have you tried a diet of dark green leafy vegetables. ..welllll you really shouldnt be soooo sad... An ice cold water plunge... I heard about this guy who... you should be grateful... did you read about... Think of this disease as a gift...you Look fine! ... Maybe there was a lesson you needed to learn... other people have it worse you know...AND one thing that so many of us with MS can have in common is how damn invisible we've become. and when people give these suggestions! it becomes all about them & what they think they know & YOU now feel even more invisible IF! somebody tells you they have multiple sclerosis... just. listen. let them know , That to you, at least in that moment, that they are not invisible AND! I was in so much pain. Everywhere! And the seizures! And The pain! and my hand it couldn't work. My foot was uncontrollable and my eyes and I couldn't walk and ...I was in so much pain lying under my covers and I opened up my phone and saw there was a woman in town who needed winter coats for her kids, and my kids had outgrown theirs. So... I told her how proud I was of her for asking for help cause I know how hard that is to ask...so that maybe someone could help her. No one could help me. I was incurable. Invisible. BUT. I thought I could help other people. I hoped i could. Another day, another woman & i connected her to the help she needed. I thought I could and I did AND it was like she was leaning into the sun a little bit, and I saw her, and I decided to lean into the sun with her, and The woman -the coats, leaning into the sun. It was like we were all saying, OK now it's Covid and everything is locked down and we're all kind of stuck, but let's lean into the sun together. Right ? I wanted to help people, I hoped I could. I didn't know how but I thought maybe I could. But!

I couldn't find the people who needed help. And I thought if it was so hard for me to find the people who needed help, then the people who needed it were having a hard time finding it SO! I created We Are Montclair on Facebook and instagram -the logo- this picture of me holding my children's hands-on our NOT last vacation together. I created this site to help people who had invisible problems -I helped them become a little less invisible. I created this to somehow be seen myself(?) I created this out of desperation to find something I COULD do, to help people, to be kind to people, That I could do AND I helped so many and people & businesses, organizations in town helped me help. And all of us together we just leaned into the sun together, right?, We all just leaned into the sun. I've created this sort of community, online- at my events, in person, this community of people who understand the importance of community. The importance of Kindness. People who want to come together and support each other and value each other and be valued by others... To be seen...AND! I hope that you'll come away from my story having a small sense of what it was like to grow up here in my magical Montclair. & I hope you'll come away from this with a little bit of knowledge about multiple sclerosis. AND!

I hope you'll look up We Are Montclair on instagram and follow and grow with me. I don't know what's next for me. Or how We Are Montclair will grow from here. It's something really special & I'm really proud of what I've done and I hope you'll all just come and lean into the sun... with me.

You should probably go buy a bunch from this site. It's a great idea.

http://ThisIsAGreatIdea.etsy.com

Photo credit for this picture as well as the cover photo: Celestina Ando.

CHAPTER TWENTY-FOUR

Rose Gold & Lizzie

When I was growing up, my best friend Andrea had two little sisters. They were like my sisters too. The three of them would often argue and I would be called in as the mediator. If one of them got in trouble in school, the office would call me down to help deal with the situation. When they heard a strange noise in the house late at night, they'd call me. My dad yelled at Andrea once and told her to call the police if she was scared. But I never minded. When they'd go out to buy school clothes, their mom would make sure I was there too. When I'd run away from home, I'd walk into their house without knocking, and greet their dad in the kitchen, which was the first room you'd pass when you entered from the driveway.

He'd ask me if I was running away again and I'd say yes, and he'd sit me down at the kitchen table and we'd talk and we'd joke and he'd tell me stories and we'd eat and we'd eat. They're Italian and they always had a house full of delicious food. Main dishes, side dishes, snacks, desserts, breads, cheeses... it was great at all times. And they always wanted me to eat. When we'd go out to Long Island to visit with their Grandma Lily, the routine was the same. Sit down and eat, eat, eat. I never minded. Often, I'd be sitting with their dad for hours before any of them knew I was there. When someone would appear in the kitchen, he'd tell them that I'd run away again and everyone would file in and sit down and we'd eat. All of us would sit down and eat and we were family. They were my second parents and I was grateful for them. Their door was always open to me in every way. They made me feel safe and included and funny and capable and smart. They made me feel loved. And when their mom suddenly died, I was called.

"My mom's dead!! My mom's dead!! You have to come over!! MY MOM IS DEAD!!!!!". It was our senior year of high school, right before prom. May 16, 1989. So I asked my mom to please drive me. I usually walked to their house, but it was urgent and the walk there was all the way across town. It took time. It would've taken too long. They needed me and what was going on?! What happened?! Wasn't she fine when I saw her last week? What happened?! My mom dropped me off and I ran to Andrea, who was pacing in the driveway and trying so hard to breathe. And when I ran into the kitchen, I found their dad there. He hugged me so tightly and we cried and we cried and he kept repeating the word Why. Over and over through his sobbing, he kept asking the world Why. I had no answers.

And when an adult who was there told Lizzie, the youngest sister, that she had to be tough and stop crying, I screamed at that woman in my Lizzie's defense. I told them all that they should cry as much as they wanted and that I would defend them against anyone who hurt their feelings. And so I would go over after school to help the younger one's with their homework. And we'd make popcorn with spices and we'd jump on the couches and we'd watch movies and we'd eat and we'd eat. And after their dad was taken away in handcuffs, I was there for the trial.

He was NOT arrested in any connection to their mother's death. But I'll leave it at that because Andrea's writing her book now and that's her story to tell. I will share that when he was sentenced, I was there for the verdict. When he was locked up in Lake Placid, I went with them to visit. And since they now didn't have parents to take care of them, I created the paperwork for my parents to become their guardians. They became my foster sisters. They were my sisters. We were family and time passed. Their mom had died, Grandma Lily had died, their dad was away for a very long time, and my Lizzie was diagnosed with cancer.

My Lizzie had cancer. My Lizzie who I'd known since she was a baby. I was so young when we met that I don't remember my life before there was a Lizzie. And my Lizzie's poor body was in so much pain and I would regularly send her gift certificates for massages. And she was so sweet and so thankful. She could've purchased her own massages, but that wasn't the point. I wanted her to literally feel me wanting to help her. And she did and I'm so thankful for that. And in my office one day, someone brought a flower delivery to me. It was a beautiful, beautiful bouquet of my favorite, yellow daffodils. On a Tuesday, with no holiday in sight, I opened the card and it was from Elizabeth. And it read, "You are a wonderful person. You are a magnificent mother. You make this world better. And I don't think you hear that enough." And I will never forget those flowers. I will never forget that note. The way those flowers and that message and her thoughts and her love felt; I will hold onto it all, forever.

When she was alive, I always interchangeably called her Lizzie and Elizabeth, so I see no need to change that in my writing. And when my Lizzie was going through chemo, she would rent a car and drive from her place in New York to mine in New Jersey. First order of business was lunch. Then, directly over to the L'Oreal Company store, so she could use my friends and family discount. She always came with a very well researched list of items to buy. We got 50% off retail at that store with my company ID! I had no idea how many brands I loved, fall under the L'Oreal umbrella until I started working there. That company store was incredible. And as employees, every two months we'd get money to spend in the store, which was a highlight for most. We loved our "free goods".

The ability to get so many high quality products for free is definitely something I miss from my time there. It was cool too, because I worked on so many of those product lines. Claims on them were created with my guidance. Commercials for these products aired because of my close work with the television networks. When I did product liability work, these products were some that a I'd successfully defended. I knew the high quality of these products because I'd seen the scientific data, the consumer studies, the criteria for these studies to be valid. I wrote dossiers that were submitted to all of the television networks to explain and confirm and persuade and ensure that our products were seen. I spoke with scientists and marketers and doctors and lawyers and I wrote dossiers that could be 3 pages or 300, depending on what was needed. Commercials were aired because of what I communicated in my writing and because of what I communicated when I spoke. Dossiers that I wrote were used by other L'Oreal Claims Departments throughout the world. I worked hard and I did a good job. I'm glad I got those free goods.

Because I'm worth it.

So after her car was packed with her L'Oreal haul, we'd head to my house to paint. When I had bought my home, I painted every room and every wall myself. I'd get home from a day at the firm where I worked, I'd stay up late and play music and paint. I had created and painted a fairy Princess themed bedroom at my daughter's request and now that I was pregnant again, I decided to create a nature scene for my son's bedroom. After looking through websites for days, I came across a site that sold stencil kits for painting room designs. I wasn't sure which one to choose until I came across a stencil that could be included. They showed an example a finished version of the room and that included the sign that had "Jacob", my son's name on it. So I was sold. It was a sign. And so after the company store trips, Elizabeth and I would go to my soon to be son's bedroom, open all of the windows for ventilation, and paint. We'd paint my son's room together while my daughter would nap with her princesses in the room next door.

Each month, Lizzie and I would add a little more. We started when I was 5 months pregnant and she was undergoing chemo for her first battle with cancer. We wouldn't play any music or have a tv on and for the most part, we didn't talk. We painted in silence. Not because we planned it that way, but because we didn't need to speak to hear each other. And the way we painted was as if it was a fully rehearsed scene from a play. I would paint the body of the bird and then I would move on to a cloud. She would be painting the owl and then on to paint the wings, so my bird could fly. Then she would paint the trunk of the tree and then I would paint the branches. It went on like this each time. No rehearsal, it just was what it was. When it was all painted, as a final touch, we placed a stencil above the door that read, "p.s. I love you". We felt it and that will always stay above that door. Lizzie said we should create a business painting rooms like we did for Jacob. When she got better, we'd go into business doing this thing we loved to do together and that created such a beautiful result. We thought a lot about the name and the marketing. We decided that when she got better, we'd make it happen and we'd be really happy and successful and we'd call our business "The Surviver Sisters". We were both survivors, for different reasons, and we were sisters with a business we were ready to create. The Survivor Sisters. That was the plan for when she survived.

When I shared on my social media page that I was struggling through some issues with multiple sclerosis, a woman named Rosie reached out to me. She owns a place called Rose Gold Wellness on South Fullerton Ave. She has acupuncture and cupping and all sorts of treatments that are holistic, Wellness treatments. Real ones, not snake oil. I felt her reaching out to me was very authentic and so I responded and I'm glad that I did. The more time I spent around Rosie getting acupuncture and massage and cupping... The more I learned about her. The more I learned about her passion for helping others.

I learned that she has chosen to not only run her business and help people that way, but also to work a great deal with people in hospice. And I asked her. I asked her how she could live with that grief of losing someone who she had cared for. It has been ten years since my Elizabeth died and that grief clings so tightly to me. Rosie told me how rewarding it was for her to help somebody in their last days. Help them to find some comfort. She told me that someone she cared for in hospice recently died and that it was incredibly painful and that she cried; and that she let herself cry and feel it. She told me it's the most painful part of her work and it's also the most rewarding. That she couldn't have that reward if she didn't have that pain. And I asked her, how you can possibly come to terms with losing somebody you cared for so much. And then she said these words... She said, "I am sad that she died. And I am glad that she lived. And I am glad that I knew her." And as she said those words, I felt my Elizabeth with me. I felt her there with me.

My Lizzie. I saw her so clearly in my mind as if she were right there. I saw her with the hairstyle that I'd only seen her wear once before with makeup she wore for an interview she gave a couple of years before she died. She was looking very serious, but not unhappy. Pensive. Concerned maybe? And in my mind, I said to her, "OK! I really like this look!! We're going with this look these days!" and I felt her smiling back at me. It felt like, I felt her smile. It felt so natural, like we just happened to bump into each other there. In my mind I told her that I loved her look and that I was so happy to see her. She smiled and she didn't look concerned anymore. Not a big huge smile, but a smile of understanding maybe? A smile of love. I felt that part in the way I felt her looking at me. I felt her love in the look. It was like we were having a conversation. I can't explain it better but I swear to you, I felt her smiling with me. And with those words that Rosie said, "I am glad that she lived. And I am glad that I knew her". It was like this whole past decade of horrible, intense grief over losing my Lizzie... It was like it was lifted. It was like... OK. I am ready now. I am ready to not to be torn up by her absence. I am ready to take a deep breath and say "I am glad that she lived. And I am glad that I knew her". It is true. My Elizabeth. I am glad that you lived. And I am glad that I knew you.

Thank you, Rosie.

Us

Always at that table eating.

High school days. Andrea Jenny &
Me. Andrea knows her eyes are
closed but we couldn't find another
picture from this night so we're us-
ing it and she's beautiful no matter
what. Great eyeshadow.

Lizzie's NYC wedding. I was 5 months
pregnant with my son. Her hair held on
for the wedding & fell out the next day.
One of her dreams was to survive long
enough to hold my Jacob.

T-shirts I had made for a bunch of
us. She created a blog with this as
the title.

The walls we painted together

Her hair was gone and so she
bought this wig to wear to my son's
baby shower. Our lifelong friend
Jenny was there too. Jenny always
shows up. I am grateful for her.

friends forever

The incredible diaper cake Elizabeth made.

My daughter and I took her to see Cin-
derella on Broadway, in honor of the 5th
month of pregnancy with her daughter
Lily.

Elizabeth talking with my Sarah about life and love and family.

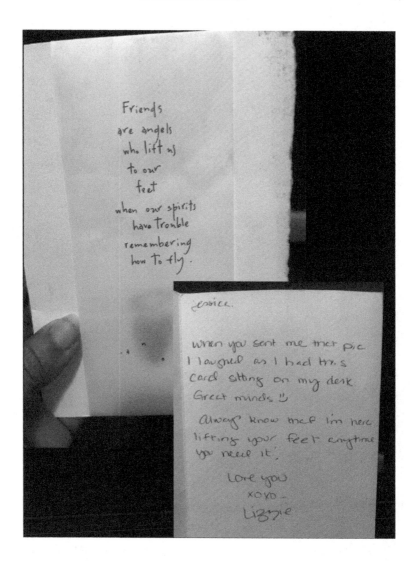

Each friend represents a world in us, a world possibly not born until they arrive, and it is only by this meeting that a new world is born. (Anais Nin)

She got to hold my Jacob.

CHAPTER TWENTY-FIVE

Eyeballs and Oreos

Where you're from and how you were raised, matters. I've referenced a bit, though I haven't shared yet that I was raised by my father, who is an eye doctor and surgeon. And by my mother who is a psychiatric social worker and a teacher later in life. And my surgeon father was also an incredible chef. And my social worker/teacher Mom, was also an incredible bad ass hippie. Short shorts, crop tops, peace signs, flowers in the hair... I say with pride that she was a hippie.

So in our family room on our big TV would be an up close image of an eyeball being stitched, accompanied by my father's voice. My dad would review the surgeries he had done while my mom would sit nearby with her eyes closed, breathing in through her nose and out through her mouth, moving her body in ways that were right for her. Which I learned later in life, was called yoga. I just knew it all as movements that you do to make your body feel better, to feel good, energized, to feel balanced. And when we would meditate, my mantra, my word was "Oreos". Because we were told to think of a word that brought us peace and joy and we were never allowed to eat Oreos in my family. We never had any junk food or sugar cereal or candy. We certainly never had Oreos and I dreamed of them, as children do about such things. I would sit there and close my eyes and say "Oreos. Oreos. Oreos." As I'm writing I'm thinking I might try again. The Oreos thing I mean. But that's not the point.

The point is that I was raised by very complex people who both lived their lives guided firmly by Eastern and Western medicine. The scientific and the mystical. The baby cobra and the sutured eyeball. That's how I was raised. And when I see people claiming to be "yogis", claiming to be "enlightened" because it's a fad to some... none of this stuff is new to me. And it can irritate me when people think of it as more of a business than a way of living or a way of truly helping others. When they use what could be beautiful, as an excuse to judge and critique others. Someone told me once I wasn't enlightened enough, because I had no interest in their fakakta suggestions. Nope. I don't want to inject any frog venom into my veins that might make me numb and cause me a lot of pain and leave me vomiting. No. I don't. And it's not because you're more enlightened than anyone, ever. It's because that's bat-shit, crazy and why don't you leave those frogs in the Amazon alone. Colonizer. But that's not the point.

It's that when I'm angry or sad or frustrated, I often know how to turn that energy around for myself. Which is the kind of thing I think that people are referring to when they talk about Reiki. Which is just another example of... I don't have a name for it. I just know it and I know how to do it. I know how to allow myself to feel what I need to feel. I have specific stretches and movements and dances that probably all have names but to me they're just the way my body moves when that's the way it needs to. All honesty, I've never found a yoga class that I like and I think it's because it wasn't a "class" for me when I was growing up. It was part of everyday life.

Although there was a class that I loved. At the Women's Commonwealth Club in my town, where my mom used to go to take exercise classes. And I loved going with her. I didn't participate, it was just for adults. It was during that time in the 70s and 80s, when women wore the exercise outfits consisting of legwarmers and matching arm warmers and headbands and leotards and tights... You know what I mean? Can you see it? And in the back of the room were folding tables where they would have pamphlets or whatever. I would go and I would hide underneath. And I would watch them and for me it was like I was watching a Broadway show. They all had these amazing outfits! They all knew the exercise routines, so they moved in unison. It was magical. I would sit underneath that table and watch those ladies dance in their legwarmers and their matching headbands... I can hear Sheena Easton right now. "My baby takes the morning train...". I can see the moves and I can see my mom. Happy. My hippie happy mom. I can see her dancing. Years later, when I heard the song "I hope you dance" by Leanne Womack, I knew that would always be my song for her. I sang it to her a lot. I'm proud of my mom.

And my dad would create masterpieces in the kitchen, from one cuisine to the next. We baked bread and made homemade pasta. He'd call for help from the kitchen and I'd arrive to find he needed help tasting the whipped cream he'd just made for the ice cream that would be that night's dessert. And of course, he'd made the ice cream too. When my stuffed animals got old and needed TLC, my dad the surgeon was always on the job. And at bedtime, he could weave a tale better than anyone; he often created fantastic adventures on the spot that left his kids the heroes every time. He had one repeating character in his stories who always helped save the day. When I had kids he told me that the character was now mine. So I've told my kids lots of stories with that magical creature, and they've had lots of adventures created by me. They are the heroes now.

My parents inspired in me, my love of dancing, baking, my love of moving, cooking, my love of mindfulness, story-telling, picture-taking, learning, my love of religion and nature and love in my faith, my love of healthy food, and analytical thinking, my love of reading, helping others and of being kind. I will always remember them for all of these things. I am grateful for all these things.

And when we were home, in addition to the few shows we were allowed to watch unsupervised, we would watch TV together as a family sometimes. We'd watch the Cosby show and Silver Spoons and MASH, which I really didn't understand. Punky Brewster and Different Strokes and The Facts of Life. Magnum PI, The Rockford Files, the A-Team. Dukes of Hazard. Dynasty and Dallas. I absorbed every minute. I loved watching the actors act and seeing them become these people on screen. I'd imagine myself there all of the time. I didn't always understand all of the shows but I still loved being absorbed in their acting.

And I didn't always know when my parents were paying attention to the shows; my mom always, always, Always had a book with her. My daughter is that way; always reading. But I always knew she was watching when "Family Ties" came on. Cause whenever it would start, my mom would sing along with the theme song. I can hear her, " What would we do, baby, without us? What would we do, baby, without us? Cause there ain't no nothing we can't love each other through. What would we do, baby? Without us? Sha-nah-nah-nahhhhh". All together we'd all do the, "Sha-nah-nah-nahhhhh". I can see us and I can see my mom so happily and So Passionately singing to my dad. To us. Dancing and singing. What would we do baby, without us? I never wondered. Cause there ain't no nothing we can't love each other through. We sang it to each other weekly. What would we do baby, without us. I never wondered. Not even for a minute.

My parents were highly educated, highly intelligent, monetarily successful New Yorkers, who moved to New Jersey to raise their family. We were never allowed to say that we were from New Jersey. Because we weren't, but also because it was like, my parents felt that even if they moved, they were New Yorkers for life, so their kids just had to sort of have it grandfathered in. I was born in Manhattan and we lived in Brooklyn Heights and I was happy to play along and stay a New Yorker; even when we moved to New Jersey. And on weekends we would drive into New York. We would go to Broadway shows, ballet at Lincoln Center, symphonies. Museum after museum and The Nutcracker every winter; I miss going to The Nutcracker every winter. We'd get dressed up and we'd look so regal. I was in love with it all. My mom would read to us that book Eloise. You know, about the little girl who lived in the Plaza? Sometimes we would go into New York and stay there for a night or two. We'd go see a show, listen to jazz, check out a neighborhood, dinner at Lutece or Dim Sum at The Golden Unicorn. I loved every adventure, every time.

There are so many Broadway shows I saw over and over, weekend after weekend. 42nd Street. Dancin'. We were supposed to see Andy Gibb in Joseph

and the Technicolor Dreamcoat, but his understudy was there that day. We saw
Yul Brenner in The King and I. Sandy Duncan in Peter Pan and I got to meet
her after the show! We had "Little People Concerts" at Lincoln Center, with
Maestro Dino Anagnost. We got to have lunch with him and he taught us so
much about music, instruments and composing. And as an adult, I've instilled
all of this love of art in my children. We've seen "Wicked" and "The Lion King"
and "Beautiful" and... So many. And I met Monk! aka Tony Shaloub, after I
saw him in "The Bands Visit". Oh! And I saw Paul Rudd and I think, Helen
Hunt and Kyra Sedgewick in Shakespeare's "Twelfth night". And Nathan Lane
and Mathew Broderick in the "Producers"; I had front row seats! I met Bryan
Cranston and Tony Goldwyn after I saw them in "Network". It was Bryan's
birthday and we sang to him and I have pictures of him holding my hand. Yup.
That happened. Oh! And I saw the Bacon Brothers in concert and Kyra was
dancing and singing along and it was cool to see how much they really do dig
each other. But that's Too much information and that's not the point.

The point is that because my parents had done so well and worked so
hard, we had a very fortunate life. And they always wanted to be sure that we
knew that it was our responsibility to help others in this world. Tikkun Olam.
Especially because we were so fortunate to have so much. So we regularly went to
homeless shelters where I read to and played with children. We would go to food
pantries and serve; we served a lot of Christmas dinners at food pantries. We'd go
to senior facilities and play games. I formed a singing group with some friends
and we'd perform at nursing homes. And I've continued this all throughout my
life. My parents instilled that in me. I will always thank them for that. And I
have instilled it all in my children, as they will someday in theirs.

Nobody's childhood is perfect. But I think, for the most part, we're all
doing the best that we can. I'm doing the best that I can. Sometimes, I look at
my kids and say "send me the bill", jokingly referring to that time in the future
when we realize I've done something terribly wrong; I don't want them to have
to pay for my mis-steps. So I tell them to send me the bill. I'm doing the best I
can. And they know that. My children are loved and valued, and appreciated and
cherished and adored and respected and they know it all. They know it because I

show them. And they know it because I tell them. Every single day, my children know how much they are loved by their mama. They will never have cause to doubt it. As long as I'm alive, my children will always know my arms will always be open to them. I am thankful that I have given them this life. I am thankful that I have given them all of this love. Where you're from and how you were raised, matters.

CHAPTER TWENTY-SIX

Some details and unequivocal proof

Singing "In the good old Summertime" at the Van Dyke Nursing Home that used to be on North Mountain. Heidi was singing with me. She was a good friend. When kids wouldn't play with me because my skin is brown, Heidi refused to play with them ever again. She was a good friend. We watched Fraggle Rock together. And she was in my singing group. Heidi is no longer with us. I am glad that she lived. And I am glad that I knew her.

Yup. All of this happened. Yup. Do you see that Bryan Cranston is holding my hand? DO YOU?! Look again. See it! Yup. That happened.

While we're at it, let's look at more pictures of the incredible famous people I've met. The only one in that picture compilation that I didn't meet in my fabulous town, is Willie Mays. Did I write about being in a commercial with him? You know, "The Say Hey Kid"! He was nice to my little sister. I liked him. Everyone in these pictures was kind. Even the photographer for the background picture of me in my boots, is based in Montclair. Her name is Celestina Ando and she's on Park Street. There are a bunch of pictures near the end that she took as well; the four pix that have a professional look and black/grey background are from her. But don't go there now cause it's better to read in order. That photo session with Celestina was my birthday gift to myself last year. And ok, so there's Nissim Black who was at the Wellmont Plaza, brought to town by Chabad Montclair. Kwame Alexander with the town's Literary Festival. Norm Lewis with The Vanguard Theater. And Patrick Wilson & Dagmara Dominczyk at The Clairidge Theater. I only said hello to them for a quick minute but their kindness to each other grabbed me. He was in the audience & she was the moderator & he was totally digging everything she had to say. He was crushin hard. It's so nice to see married people who really like and appreciate each other. They reminded me of Kyra and Kevin. I'm only 4 degrees from Kevin Bacon. Here's how: The fabulous physical trainer I worked with every week before I got sick, is Shakiem Evans. Check him out on instagram @XByShakiemEvans. You want to take his class. Trust that. So he was in "The Other Guys" with Will Ferrell who was in The Campaign with John Lithgow who was in Footloose with Kevin Bacon. It's really like Kevin and Kyra and I are family at this point. Have you heard music by the Bacon Brothers? I love every song. Check them out if you haven't already. TMI is my favorite.

The hot pink Louboutin Boots are mine of course. The other shoes belong to Dagmara and Molly Ringwald!! I got so many pictures up close! But the angle was bad and none of my pictures of them were flattering enough to share. Girl Code ya'll. So I cropped the pix and kept the shoes cause look- PROOF!! I met Molly Ringwald. It's proof. Trust me, I'm a lawyer. And a Doctor in Australia. Maybe. I don't actually know if that's true. But I read it on the internet, so it must be true. When I met Molly Ringwald I wanted to say something clever to her but instead I just said, "I like pink" a couple of times. Maybe something about my boots. I don't know. I've had more eloquent moments. But I do like pink and I was wearing boots, so there's that.

That Muppet Song "Mah Na Mah Na" just came onto my playlist and I took a quick break to dance with my kids. And our dog. We put it on repeat for about 10 minutes and it was so much fun. But I digress... But wait, go listen to it and dance for a few minutes. If you let yourself get weird with it, it's a really great song to dance to. Let it get weird.

And Definitely sing along. It will be relatively easy to pick up on the lyrics. There should be a lot of arm movement. Think Steve Martin in "The Jerk". Or wild and crazy with Dan Aykroyd. Or Ed Grimley! I think it's illegal in the United States and Canada, to mention Steve Martin without mentioning Martin Short. Maybe Mexico too, I'll google it. Have you seen "Only Murders in the Building"?! You must. My kids and I make a day if it and binge entire seasons in one sitting. And we love Selena Gomez. I mean, we don't know her but. You know what I mean. So go and channel all of these guys and girls and Mah Na Mah Na for ten minutes. 5? I don't want to step on your creative process. You do you. Go for it. I'll wait.

CHAPTER TWENTY-SEVEN

Lawn Parties and UCLA

So time did what it does, I went someplace for undergrad for my first year and wasn't happy there. So I transferred to University of Maryland's Best Campus. UMBC. Or UCLA. Which stands for University of Catonsville, Left of Arbutus. It's a geography joke. Not actually funny, and perhaps only briefly amusing if you went there. But that's not the point.

I went there and I loved it. University of Maryland Baltimore County. I was really, really happy there. There was a campus television show called. "U Must Be Crazy" and I was one of the stars of the show. And one of the producers. And one of the writers. I loved it. People would gather in the main lobby area in the dorms and watch the episodes of the show and I just couldn't bear to watch myself on camera in front of other people. So I never actually saw myself on that show, and sometimes I wonder if any recordings of it still exist. We interviewed people on campus, for their events, for volunteer opportunities.

I participated in so many volunteer oppportunities too. Like "paddle for people" where we got sponsors for paddle boating at the Inner Harbor. We raised money to help heat the homes of people in Baltimore who couldn't afford heat in the winters. I was proud of that. I am proud of that. Tikkun Olam. I'll never know who I helped but I know that I did. There were people in Baltimore who were warm that winter, because of me. Because I cared and because I tried and that still warms me now.

I loved my time at UMBC. I was happy and safe and cared for and I felt free. I remember walking past the student center one evening with Andrea. A guy came running out, with a guitar strapped over his shoulder. He ran up to me, looked at me very intently and shouted, "Perfect! Follow me inside!!" and he turned back to run into the student center. So Andrea and I shrugged and laughed and went inside. We opened the door to see the "Perfect! Follow me inside!!" guy, surrounded by several other guys, who all had instruments too. And as the door closed behind us, the guys all began to sing. "Brown eyed girl" by Van Morrison. I didn't know any of them and never saw them again and I'll always remember it all.

I worked as a Student Peer Advisor for two summers, working with incoming students; freshman and transfers and their parents. I loved that job. It was all of us Student Peer Advisors who saw Dead Again together. We did presentations on time management and stress management. We gave campus tours. We answered questions and played games. We were people who were there to guide and help and I loved that job. My time at UMBC will always bring me to smile. And, I doubt any of our work on U Must Be Crazy still exists.

What I do know still exists, thanks to the Internet and my children who are far more savvy than I am, is me at 10 years old on the Guiding Light. Did you ever see that soap opera the Guiding Light? It was on CBS at 3 o'clock. Up against General Hospital. It was like the rivals of soap operas... General Hospital versus Guiding Light. ABC versus CBS... Which one will you choose!? My older sister and my mom loved the soap operas on CBS. There was Young and the Restless followed by The Bold and the Beautiful followed by As the World Turns followed by the Guiding Light. So check this out, I was home and one of my dad's patients called and wanted to speak to my dad. It was well before the days of cell phones. I knew that my parents were a few houses down at our neighbors' house, in their backyard because they were having a lawn party.

Our neighbors were actors and were in a lot of cool stuff, like the movie Witness with Harrison Ford! And they said he was really nice and he actually helped with the set. That one day, people were looking for him, and they found him helping build; I think they said he used to be a carpenter? I'm not sure about that, but I remember they said that he was a kind, down to earth guy. That's so cool. I love hearing stories like that. So cool. But, so unbeknownst to me, there were some famous and famous-adjacent people at that party too. Well, I wanted to be sure that my father got his message so I told him I would go find my dad. It wasn't an emergency, but I knew my father cared so much about his patients, so I went to find him. I walked into their backyard where there were a lot of people milling around and I found my mom and the neighbor and they were talking to a beautiful woman with a kind smile. So I said hello to everyone and introduced myself and told my mom why I was there and she called my dad over. I gave him the message and he left to call his patient. And my mother said to me, "you're not going to believe who this person is that we're talking to". And she told me that this nice woman was a producer on the Guiding Light! My jaw absolutely dropped. I was speechless. My mom and my older sister, who I thought were two of the coolest people in the world, were in love with this show; and now I was standing in front of someone who produced it! I remember that feeling of absolute exhilaration!

I remember feeling how much I loved that this woman was powerful and that this woman was so nice. She was so kind to me. I was so in shock and so in awe and so impressed. I was saying close to nothing, but when I spoke, it was a babbling stream of I don't even know what. The woman smiled and laughed kindly and said, "How would you like to be on our Christmas show?" Yup. That. Happened.

It happened because I knew how much my dad's patients meant to him. Because I wanted to make a point of being sure that this person who needed help got help. That's why I got to be on the Guiding Light. Because I cared and I did something about it. I got to skip school, and my mom and my sister and my dad came with me. I got a present from under the Christmas tree. We're Jewish, so that was a first. It was the game of Monopoly and I loved it. Even though I don't like playing games, the symbolism of getting a gift was immense. This whole day was a gift to me and the Monopoly game was hard proof of it all. They gave me a gift! And then they gave me a check for $100!! I laughed when I saw that! I would have paid them, if I had any money, for the privilege of getting to be on television!! For getting a whole day of people being so happy I was there, so happy I was involved, so happy to see me. I couldn't believe that They were paying Me.

And I got to meet the guy who played Tony and I got to meet the man who played Josh and I got to meet the woman who played Hillary and so many other people and they were so nice and friendly and welcoming. I was 10 years old. It was one of the best days of my life. But I never had a recording of my time on that show, and I figured I never would. And I mentioned it to my kids one day. And my daughter found it online. She found me on the Guiding Light at 10 years old, in 1981. Online!!! And so I saved it or screen recorded it or whatever I did and so now I have it. And if you slow it down to the slowest speed possible, I am on camera for fifteen seconds. Fif. Teen. Whole. Seconds.

U Must Be Crazy and the Guiding Light. In terms of screen time, I haven't seen much. But those were some of the best moments of my life. I loved my time at UMBC. I was happy and safe and cared for and I felt free. I wish that time could have lasted longer but I am grateful that I had it at all. Lawn Parties and UCLA. For these things I am grateful.

Shirts for cast and crew

and the back.

Greg Beecroft "Tony", my Monopoly Gift and me

CHAPTER TWENTY-EIGHT

DC Dan and the Carabiner

I had to leave school. When I finally went back to University of Maryland, I lived in Washington DC. I didn't have any friends there and it was a very lonely time in my life. I got a job at a gift shop in Woodley Park and the manager of the store was a man named Dan. And Dan was a wonderful man. He was kind and caring and loving and gracious, and he quickly became one of the most important people to ever exist in my universe. Dan supported me and believed in me and I looked forward to going to work, just in case I'd get to work a shift with him. The only time we saw each other was there and I didn't always know in advance if I'd get to see him. Sometimes, if he wasn't working, he'd leave a little gift for me at the register and sometimes he'd leave a card. One Oscar night, he needed to be home watching the Oscars start to finish, from red carpet to ending credits, so I knew he wouldn't be at work. On the register, he left a note explaining his absence and a little plastic Oscar Meyer Wiener toy. The note ended, as many of his notes often would, "words are fluff, let's get on with the fun stuff".

I wondered sometimes if Dan had any idea how significant his presence was for me. By the time I'd returned to school and lived in DC, my world was so different. My parents had a messy divorce that went on for years; we lost our home and we lost our money. We lost our family. We went from overflowing extra tables on Thanksgiving, pool parties and fireworks, summers on my favorite place Fire Island, nightly family hangouts, weekly Shabbat dinners, vacations to beaches around the world, to Italy, the opera, the ballet... to anger, misery, sadness, and despair. It wasn't just that all of our money was gone though. It wasn't just that our home was gone either. It was that our love seemed to evaporate too. All of that magic that my parents had created turned to fury, suspicion, homelessness. My parents anger and hatred was all that seemed to matter, as our memories of love and family and happiness faded into the prologue; not even really part of our story anymore. Just a little part at the beginning. I drive past my childhood home sometimes and dream of living there again. Leaving it was such a hard goodbye and so much destruction followed for years; I don't know that anyone ever fully recovered. Divorce is a gift that can keep on giving; it has given and given and given. It has never stopped giving. My parents had loved each other and done so much good and it all exploded into the formation of enemy camps.

And while I was working every job I could get to save money to get back to school, we lived in friends' homes and then hotels and then motels on the highway. We had so much and then we were homeless; while assets were frozen and court dragged on. I slept on floors and friend's couches and in the back room of a doctor's office. I took donuts from motel lobbies to give my little brother for breakfast. I did everything in my power to keep going, to get back to school, to get myself out of this horrible life. I promised myself I'd never get

married. That I'd buy my own house and my own car and everything would be
in my name only. I'd have children and be single and my children would only
have my last name. And I'd buy a house and pay it off before my kids went to
college, so I could put the house in their names. So the house would be theirs. So
they'd know they'd always have a home. So my children would never be homeless
like I was. So no adult's anger and bad decisions could take everything they'd
ever known away from them. So I would know that my children would never
suffer the way I did. My children would never be homeless. My children could
never be homeless. Walking my dogs in the motel parking lots, I promised that
I'd create a happy, loving home, that they'd always be able to go to. I promised
that as long as I was alive, they'd never wander this earth scared and lonely and
alone. They didn't even exist yet, but I knew what their names would be and I
repeated my promises to them over and over and over.

    And so I got back to school. And I focused on getting my degree so I could
get that house and that car and never be homeless again. And I didn't have any
friends there so I was very lonely. Determined and lonely and then there was
Dan. He was kind to me. Always. Without fail. I could always count on kindness from Dan. He was hilarious and insightful. He was the best at wrapping
presents and creating bows out of ribbon. He called me Wonder Woman. He
was my sunshine.

    I thought a great deal about how I was going to get out of my sad existence in
Washington DC. I loved my neighborhood and I loved working with Dan and
that wasn't enough. The misery and sadness that I tried to escape from home
seemed to follow me there and I needed to figure out a way to walk away; to find
happiness for myself.

    One of the many things that I loved about my neighborhood was that I
could take a quick metro ride to the Washington mall and go to museums that
were free! Every chance I got, I would go to the museums and it didn't matter
what the subject was or what the focus was, if it was free, I was there. I would
wander through the rooms and read the descriptions and try to escape into the
world of the artists. I would try to see them and understand them and their
perspectives, and it would make me feel less alone. It would make me feel like I

was part of something bigger than myself, and I loved my time with those artists, in those museums.

On a day when I was heading out with someone, and wondering how to make my life better, I glanced up and saw as the light changed, the sign changed to "walk". For some reason it grabbed me, and I stood there and watched the sign blink walk. Walk. WALK. So I didn't say a word to the guy I was with, who had gone ahead of me anyway, I hailed a cab and I left. I went back to the place I was living and the place I knew I had to leave. I packed my bags, drove to UMBC and headed straight to the financial aid office.

And I asked them if they had some sort of a poor person's loan. I told them that I really wanted to finish school, but I didn't have any more money. I didn't tell them that I had gotten a job at the fitness center, so I could shower there. That I'd scoped out an area in the library where a lot of people didn't go late at night, so I could sleep there. And if it came to it, of course, I could sleep in my car. I was dreading the idea of being homeless again, but I refused to engage in a life that kept me miserable, even one more day. Walk. The sign said walk. And the job at the fitness center would give me enough money for food and gas. I just needed a loan to help me pay for my classes. I asked them to help me. They said yes. So I took out a loan which was enough to get a room on campus and pay for my classes. I had a place to stay and I was so happy I wasn't going to be homeless again. As embarrassing as it was, I went to each one of my teachers and told them that I didn't have enough money for books, that I was a good student and I wondered if they had any extras I could borrow. Each one of them said yes. I was happy and I was grateful.

For my last semester at UMBC, I rented a room in the house of a guy who also went there. It was him, two or three other guys and me. I shared a bathroom with several of them and another guy had the basement and his own bathroom. My room was so tiny, that all that fit in it was a loveseat that could open up into a small bed and a table for a television. It wasn't super comfortable when I opened it up so I would usually just leave it closed and sleep on the loveseat or on the floor. It was sort of better that way because when I opened up the loveseat, there was literally no more room in the room. I was definitely nervous about living in a house and sharing a bathroom with a bunch of guys, but it was the only thing that I could afford and I just couldn't be homeless again. And all of the guys were kind and friendly and respectful, and I was glad to be living there. A friend of mine from school liked to cook, but couldn't where she lived, so she'd bring over lots of food and we'd all barbecue and hang out and listen to music and watch movies. And she would always insist that I keep the leftovers, because she knew I didn't have enough money for food, but that I wouldn't ask. I had friends. I had a place to live. I had food sometimes. I took my classes with my borrowed books and I was grateful for all of it.

And so I graduated with a major in English and a minor in Sociology. Before I left, I went to Washington DC to check out my museums one last time. Dan met me there and we sat on one of the benches on the mall. We didn't say too much. We knew that this was sort of the end of an era; that we wouldn't be there, sitting on this bench, maybe not ever again. We didn't say much. I had no idea what was going to come next in my life. I didn't know where I'd live or what I'd become, but I had finally finished college, and I had to keep moving. I had to figure out how to make my promises to my children come true. My promises to myself. I knew I would figure out how to be ok somehow and I also knew that I was going to miss Dan so much. So we sat there for a while and we watched the world go by.

Life went on and Dan and I stayed in touch. We wrote letters. Not emails or texts. We wrote letters. Thoughtful letters. We would send each other gifts and cards. We thought about each other a lot. We loved each other and we supported each other and for 25 years, half of my life, nothing that happened to me happened without Dan knowing about it. The ups and the downs and the highs and the lows, he was my biggest supporter and my loudest cheerleader. He believed in my strength and my ability to survive. He believed in my goodness and my kind heart. He saw me for me and he loved me for me and my heart aches with his absence. Part of me is still waiting for him to come back.

Dan was an artist. He worked with Jim Henson- the Muppets! He taught at Juilliard. He was a craftsperson at the Santa Fe Opera. He could draw and paint and create everything out of anything. He was a brilliant writer. He was a brilliant friend. He was such a beautiful human being.

When I passed the bar, he sent me a carabiner. And attached to it was a note that he wrote. And the note read, "Jessica, this is a clip used in rock climbing. Let it serve as a symbol of all the mountains you've climbed. Let it remind you of the heights you can achieve when you reach beyond the stars for your dreams. Let it mark your place when the air gets thin and you need a moment to get your footing. Let it promote thoughts of the love out of which it was given. Love yourself more than anything. You deserve it. Congratulations on passing the Bar Exam! Take this clip, because... You ROCK. Love, Dan". That hangs on a hook on the wall by my bed.

All throughout my house are things that he created for me. On my family room wall is a picture I painted of him, on my stairway is a picture of him with me and one of him with my kids. We'd go to DC from time to time to see Uncle Dan and he'd send cards and gifts to my kids too.

Across from my dining room table is a picture of him and every once in a while I look up and I'm happily surprised to see him smiling at me. I loved that man. I will always love that man. Dan died in the hospital on February 9, 2022. I miss him terribly. I am glad that he lived. And I'm glad that I knew him. And I cannot let go of this grief.

I'll end this with some of my Dan's creations that live throughout my home. No story of my life would be complete without a chapter for my DC Dan.

"*You sound like a woman running with a fistful of life in both hands. Don't trip toots!*"

The painting I did of my DC Dan

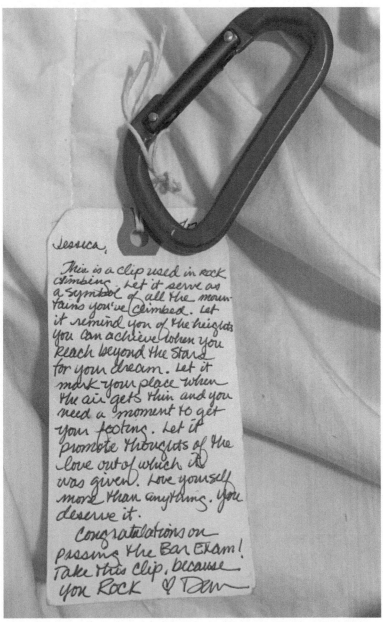

The title piece

Daniel Kessler 💜💜💜💜💜

Mar 19, 2016 · 🔒
Just arrived today from my always wonderful friend
Daniel Kessler. 💜💜💜💜💜💜💜

be brave

After the diagnosis letter and gifts from DC Dan to us. "Dear Jessica, Sarah and Jacob. Here are some reminders that even when the world seems a bit cruel and unfair, you have an amazing sense of justice, wonderful strength and a bit of magic to fight for goodness. I think the character of Wonder Woman exemplifies all of that. Sending love by the buckets. DC Dan."

Daniel Kessler shared a memory.
Favorites · Jul 23, 2017 · 🌐

Real life Wonder Woman, Jessica

6 Years Ago
See your memories ›

Jessica Lynne is with Daniel Kessler.
Jul 23, 2015 · ⚙

Thank you DC Daniel for my amazing new apron. Love you!!! 🤍🤍🤍

and without much worry, because I have
always been impressed by your outstanding
ability and amazing heart. I am counting on the
hope that this disease and the fight against it won't
change your virtue. Be as confident as you can
be,
Once again, words are fluff - let's get on with
the fun stuff. Much Love, D

...I have always been impressed by your outstanding ability and amazing heart. I am counting on the hope that this disease and the fight against it won't change your virtue. Be as confident as you can be. Once again, words are fluff. Let's get on with the fun stuff. Much Love, Dan.

CHAPTER TWENTY-NINE

What would we do, baby, without us

I n the early 1900s, William Butler Yeats wrote a poem called "The Second Coming". Broadly, it is about religion, society and the state of the world. The words that grabbed me in it were, "Things fall apart. The center cannot hold. Mere anarchy is loosed upon the world[1] ". I read it when I returned to college, and so in 1995, I felt exactly what William Butler Yeats wrote in 1919.

Because, my family. Things had fallen apart. Our center did not hold. Tragically. Our center could not hold.

In the 1950s, Chinua Achebe wrote the book "Things fall apart". His work was filled with so much power. He quoted that passage from Yeats. "The Second Coming" passage.

So back in 1958, Achebe read what Yeats wrote back in 1919. He identified with what he read. And with that, Yeats was seen. He was seen by Achebe and

---

1. Yeats, William B.. "The Second Coming." 1920.

he was seen by all of Achebe's readers. And now, they're both seen by you. So much power in the written word.

Cause in 2024, I wrote about 1995, when I read Achebe from 1958, and we both read Yeats from 1919 and now you are reading about it all. Power. So much power in words.

I saw them both and I heard them both. They were there with me. And I was there with them, as you are now here with me. They were with me, for the anarchy. Mere anarchy. That's what it felt like when my parents got divorced. Mere anarchy when we were homeless. Anarchy when I had to take donuts from the motel lobby. Anarchy when I became a survivor. Mere anarchy when I thought I was going to be sleeping in the library. Loosed upon the world. When I stopped being able to read during law school. When I was covered in bruises because I didn't know how to walk anymore. When I couldn't find my children. When I thought I was going to die. Anarchy. Anarchy. multiple sclerosis. Anarchy. These past years 6 with multiple sclerosis. Anarchy has been loosed upon my world. The center cannot hold.

All of the things. All of the things. They fell apart.

Sha-nah-nah-nahhhhh.

CHAPTER THIRTY

Pop Rocks and my left foot

As I look at the title for this chapter, I'm thinking that there was a movie called my left foot. Was there? I feel like there was and that it was with Daniel Day-Lewis? I might be making that up and I'll have to Google it later. I remember going to see my older sister at her office uptown many years ago, when she was crushing hard on Daniel Day-Lewis. And as I walked past a movie theater who had one of his movies, they had a life-size cut out of him standing in front of the theater. I walked up to the guy inside and asked if I could have it for 10 bucks and he said yes. So I put Daniel Day-Lewis underneath my arm and walked about 30 blocks across Manhattan to my sister's office.

She's a lawyer also, so where she worked was pretty stuffy, you know how lawyers are. And I was laughing uncontrollably the entire way at the looks on people's faces as I carried my buddy Daniel under my arm. In truth, I find myself to be absolutely hilarious and very, very entertaining. And the looks of confusion made the whole thing even better.

So I went inside and got my visitors pass, which I promptly placed on Mr. Day-Lewis and I went in the crowded elevator, up to her office. I knocked on the closed door and when she told me to come in, I opened it and placed my walking companion Daniel in her doorway. And then I peaked over his shoulder to see her reaction. Wait, no, I must have looked around him, cause I'm 5'6 and he's definitely taller. So I looked around him as my sister eyes went so wide and immediately her laughter began. It was so worth it. So. Worth it. I think she kept him in her office until she moved her next job. I'm guessing that when clients came in she moved him to the side, maybe behind the coats, but I truly hope that she honored Mr. Lewis. He was very good company during those 30 blocks that we spent together. But that's not the point.

The point here is that for the past, almost 2 years now, I've been steadily and increasingly losing control of my left foot. It started with one toe and then another. Then all of my toes would sort of jump around and do a little dance. It would happen so quickly that I wasn't always entirely sure that it was happening and then it became part of life so I just sort of ignored it. But then my foot. My left foot. It started twitching and turning; feeling like there were pop rocks exploding in it. Random explosions of pop rocks in my foot. And although the title is, "my left foot" it's not just in my foot anymore. It's moved up to my calf and my knee and now it's in my thigh. 24 hours per day. Seven days per week. It's like a combination of pop rocks and pins and needles. It is absolutely maddening. If I put any pressure on my foot, it increases the sensation of that stinging, popping, buzzing, and it's awful. When no one is looking, I drag my foot or hop, to help myself from feeling those increased feelings.

Once, I was working out at a great place called "Brain & Body" on Bellevue Ave. They have incredible machines that professional athletes use to train. They have workouts that help with your brain functioning and they have an ab machine that just about anyone could use. I can get a full workout in 20 minutes even on days when I'm physically struggling. As part of their warm-up session, they have a floor that vibrates. When I put my foot on that floor, it took away the sensation! It was just 15 or 20 seconds, but it was so beautiful to not feel that pop rocks, stinging, buzzing in my foot. And I cried. I cried because I had forgotten what it felt like to not feel like that. I know that I have forgotten what it feels like to not be in any pain. The only time I get relief from pain is when I'm in a pool. Swimming gives me relief, but I rarely have the opportunity to swim, so that relief is so rare. But for 15 or 20 seconds, I got a relief from that feeling in my foot. My daughter wants to be a doctor when she grows up. A large part of her desire is because she has seen how people so close to her have been mistreated and mishandled and ignored by doctors. She came up with a concept for what's going on with my foot that I think is absolutely brilliant. The pins and needles and the pop rocks sensation are like when you're foot falls asleep and then it wakes up; when you have to keep sort of shaking it around and stomping on it and waiting for a little bit of time to pass for it to wake up and for that sensation of pins and needles to stop. So basically, my daughter said that the messages from my brain just aren't getting through to my foot and the pins and needles are actually my foot trying to connect. My foot is trying to wake up. That makes sense. It's trying to wake up. It's trying to let my brain know it's ready and waiting and alert and awake. It's trying. I'm trying. And I'm hoping. And I'm managing. And I'm keeping my fingers crossed that someone, somewhere, will know how to help me.

I read about a man who had the hiccups for years and eventually committed suicide. No one could help him and he just couldn't live with that uncontrollable sensation anymore. And I understand. I will not commit suicide, but I understand.

My left foot. My toes. My calf. My knee. My thigh. Over two years, it has spread from my toes all the way up. No one knows why it's happened and no one can get it to stop and it's getting worse. Lots of doctors and medicines and physical therapy and chiropractic and acupuncture and cold plunge and massage and... And nothing. Nothing has helped. It's just getting worse. It has been two years of this. Six years of knowing I have this disease. This is worse. I'm not getting better. Pop rocks and pins and needles. It's all the time. It's all the time. And it's maddening. That alone, I believe, could drive a person insane. I can see myself so clearly, so giddy and happy as I walked uptown to my sister's office, carrying Daniel Day-Lewis under my arm. My left foot. It was all so funny. I had no idea what was to come. I had no idea that one day, that story would be a part of this story. This life sentence. It's quicksand.

CHAPTER THIRTY-ONE

Quicksand

Sitting in my therapist's office, I was thinking of and talking about my childhood. I jokingly brought up quicksand as one of those things that scared me as a kid. I put a lot into that concern as I grew up. But as I entered adulthood, I started believing that perhaps my lifelong fear of quicksand was unjustified. I don't know how many of you reading this grew up in the same time I did but, if you were born in the 70s and grew up in the 80s, quicksand played the major role in your life. You knew that if you got stuck in quicksand, that you should not wiggle, you should not try to swim out or pull yourself out on your own; because you wouldn't be able to. If you try to help yourself, you'll be suffocated and you will drown. You have to call for help without moving too much. You have to reach out for help, without making much of a move with that reach. You have to hope that somebody comes by who knows what to do in the case of quicksand. I don't even know what climate or locations are conducive to quicksand. Where are these pools of death found?! How does a person find themselves near it and how many people will happen to be walking by if you're stuck?! Are these highly traversed areas? If so, are there signs, so people don't fall in? It kind of looked like what I imagined when Westley and Buttercup were in the fire swamp. I think I'll google quicksand locations when I finish writing this chapter. I'll google to see if quicksand's even real?! It seems inconceivable.

Do you know what to do in case of quicksand? You stay still and hope somebody comes by and sees that you're drowning. You stay still and hope that somebody comes by and sees your suffocating. You stay still and hope that somebody comes by and sees that you're terrified and you want so desperately for someone to help you. Stay still. And if someone tries to help you in a way that isn't a helpful way, then you'll drown. If someone tries to help you in a way that you shouldn't be helped, you'll suffocate. Because they have to somehow find a very specific lengthy and weighted branch, to extend it out to you wherever you are in the quicksand. It needs to be long enough to reach you, wherever you are at that point. And if you're able to, if your arms are still above quicksand level, you have to grab onto that branch. And it needs to be strong enough that it won't break if you grab it. But it can't be too heavy for them to carry, and it has to be strong enough to pull your weight. And you have to be strong enough to hold on tightly as they drag you because quicksand is very thick.

You can't wiggle as they're dragging you, because you'll drown and suffocate. You have to sort of just, stay still sort of, trust the process, which feels insane, and let them pull you to safety. But, of course, the branch can break if the one they picked, wasn't strong enough. Of course the branch might not have been long enough to reach you in the first place. They might've misjudged how long it needed to be to get to you. And they might've misjudged how strong the branch was. Or they might've misjudged how strong you are. Or they might've misjudged how thick the quicksand is. And you have to stay still, and trust this insanity. Because if you try to get out, you'll drown. You'll suffocate. You have to stay still and hope that the person that sees that you're drowning and suffocating is strong enough and smart enough and has enough judgment to help you get the hell out. Cause you've been alone in that quicksand for a few minutes, then hours, then days, then Years. Suddenly it's been Years. It moves so quickly to years. Years with no change. Years. Stuck. Alone. Drowning. Slowly suffocating. Do you understand the level of desperation a person must feel being stuck in quicksand. Their fear. Their anguish. Their shame for having falling in it in the first place. Their confusion about where this quicksand came from anyway. The desperation.

I was diagnosed with multiple sclerosis six Years ago and my fears have been validated. No need for that google search. It's real. I'm still hoping someone will find me.

CHAPTER THIRTY-TWO

Neurologist Batman and Tony Stark

I have seen and heard and been told and been through so much nonsense since this diagnosis. I've been spoken to like I'm an idiot or like I'm an unintelligent little kid. As if I'm not a fully formed adult. The diagnosis of multiple sclerosis leads so many "healthcare" "professionals" to treat people like they're stupid and they fill patients lives with nonsense.

Nonsense like this one neurologist who sometimes put gel on my head and what seemed like a shower cap with holes and had me look at a screen and click buttons. And whose office regularly charged me for missed appointments, when they were the ones who weren't there. And this one neurologist guy ... this guy looked like a villain. Straight out of a movie. Every time he walked in the room, he had this look on his face that was so cagey that if someone said, "Oh, that guy? He's been up late in his secret underground lair working on a new poisonous concoction so he can take over the world", I'd say, "Yeah. That checks out".

When he'd walk in, I'd say hello to him by name, but in my mind, I called him "Neurologist Batman". Not like he was Batman and also a neurologist.

But like the next chapter in a Batman movie and his arch nemesis is this crazy neurologist who concocts stuff in his underground lair. And in my mind the Batman was always Michael Keaton. While I loved all of the Batmans, for some reason, Batman neurologist always starred Michael Keaton. George Clooney was great and Ben Affleck was awesome... all of them. Loved them and believed them all. And if you think by this that I'm saying that anyone could ever replace Robert Downey Jr. as Tony Stark, then you are horrifyingly, shockingly off base and I'll thank you to just reign it in. He's the only one for the job and that conversation is over.

I do love the Iron Man movies. Remember when he was in that cave and he had to do all that work, even though he was hurt!? Oh man, and when his house exploded? I loved that house. I'm getting loopy. It's 2a.m. and I'm crazy tired. My kids and I went to visit Far Brook, my incredible middle school, and it was wonderful. My teachers remembered me. They remembered that I had the lead role as Prospero in our 8th grade production of The Tempest, that I loved our ski trips, that I sang in Pergolisi's Stabat Mater, that I played the clarinet. It felt nice that they remembered me. I saw some old friends and the whole day made me feel good. And I'm tired. So I'll keep writing tomorrow. I don't even know what I'm talking about anymore. It's hard to stop writing, but I'm so tired. Goodnight. Good morning? Wakanda Forever.

CHAPTER THIRTY-THREE

Let's meet some of the doctors

I know you've met some of them too.

Dr Glazed and Confused

Dr. Here's some Oxy

Dr. This disease doesn't hurt

Dr. Maybe see a physical therapist

Dr. You need a therapist therapist

Dr. If you show me you're sad or angry or scared, I'll pat you gently on the head and smile cause you're being such an emotional little girl.

Dr. My ego won't let me admit I don't know what to do

Dr. My ego won't let me tell you I'm sorry I can't help you

Dr. I forgot that **I** work for **you**

Dr. Come in late at night to get a brain scan tonight so I can see if you urgently need medication before I leave on vacation tomorrow - and oops I forgot to call before I left on vacation

Dr. I forgot I'm in a customer service business

Dr. I know I didn't call you back when you called and said you were writhing on the floor in excruciating pain. But you're fine now so what's the problem.

Dr. I don't know just take these pills

Dr. Why do you ask so many questions

Dr. It doesn't matter that you're paying money to a babysitter so you could have this appointment with me that I said I'd take. I'm taking a long lunch. You can wait.

Dr. I'm pretty sure that I am the most fascinating insightful erudite human you've ever met, and I think I'll tell you stories to confirm those beliefs the whole time you're here

Dr. I don't need to look you in the eye

Dr. I'll take phone calls and respond to emails while you're speaking.

Dr. You've lost the right to be treated with respect.

Dr. You've lost the right to want to understand what's happening to your own body

Dr. Why haven't you realized you're becoming invisible to everyone

Dr. If you get a copy of your chart you'll see I wrote that you take too much time.

Dr. I'll tell you to your face that you're taking too much of my time

Dr. I know you just told the nurse all of your sadness and fears and concerns and questions and you watched them write it down and so, yeah. What brings you in today?

Dr. My boss needs numbers of patients and good feedback surveys & you're not helping me & my quotas

Dr. There are people waiting who I can help, so can *you*, just leave

Dr. Could we speed this up, I've really gotta fly

Dr. I can't help you and I'm not gonna try

CHAPTER THIRTY-FOUR

Often

I've read extensively that depression and suicide and thoughts of suicide are major concerns for people with multiple sclerosis. Is it accurate that people with multiple sclerosis are so distraught that they think of suicide? Do they think of it often? Yes. And yes.

And while the disease itself can be a driving force behind those emotions, there is something equally if not more significant in the role of the misery for many with MS. It is absolutely equal to the misery for me. And that is the way we are treated by too many of those in the health "care" community. Yes, I have worked with good doctors and actual healthcare professionals who care and are competent and kind. Yes, I've worked with people I'd happily see again. Yes, I am grateful for them. And yes, those people are the exceptions, not the rule.

I've intentionally not included names or identifying details for people or places. While I can't imagine anyone I've referenced ever reading this, calling out any one individual is not the point. There are a lot of horrible problems in our healthcare system and you don't need multiple sclerosis to know that. This book is not to slam or shame anyone and if you've done right by me, then you know this isn't about you and I wish you well.

This is about how it has been sadly and angeringly remarkable for me to watch my importance, my value, my dignity, my right to privacy... all wash away with the words multiple sclerosis.

You know those dreams that are so powerful when you're asleep and so impactful when you're just waking up, and then within moments of true awakening they've slipped away without a tangible sense-memory of their substance and meaning. Those dreams you have to fight to try to hold onto. Those dreams that you sort of remember as you start to get up and ready for the day, but that are then just gone and there's no way you can even begin to decipher what they were about and why it meant so much? Why it made so much sense? But the dreams are gone and you can't feel them anymore. And you can't understand why. Those fleeting memories are simply gone.

That's how I remember the way my life used to be. The way people used to speak to me. The way doctors looked at me and treated me like what was happening to me mattered. I wish I could feel that again. I wish it wasn't all like a dream. I remember compassion. I remember dignity. I remember when I mattered.

And I have the rest of my life to feel irrelevant. For my pain to be dismissed. For doctors to ignore me.

This disease is incurable. I have the rest of my life this way. The rest of my life.

Yes. People with multiple sclerosis are often depressed. People with multiple sclerosis often think of suicide.

Often.

CHAPTER THIRTY-FIVE

Keith Morrison and Lily's Sweet Shop

When I was out with my kids a bit ago driving in town, we both thought that we saw Keith Morrison. You know, that guy that Bill Hader does the impression of so brilliantly? Oh my gosh, I have such a crush on that guy. Bill Hader, I mean. But not if he's still in a relationship with Ali Wong. Because she's fantastic and I'm not trying to get in the middle of the relationship OK? I'm just saying. Oh wait. Maybe he was dating Anne Hathaway? Anna Kendrick? I'm not very good with keeping up with what celebrities do. Largely because it's none of my business. And also because, no that's really the only reason. It's none of my business. But I'm madly in love with all of those people in totally platonic, non-stalker, I'm just impressed with your talent, kind of ways.

There's a guy who I follow on my social media page who does the hair for Anne Hathaway. His name is Orlando and his work is fantastic and every single time he posts something about something he's done with Anne Hathaway, and she's smiling, I'm pretty sure that she smiling at me. But like, not in a crazy person way. Not that I'm saying she's crazy. I'm saying that I'm not crazy.

Methinks she doth protest too much. I fell in love with Shakespeare at Far Brook. I absolutely love Shakespeare. But that's not the point.

So my kids and I thought that we saw Keith Morrison and I shouted his name out of the car window, which my kids thought was absolutely hilarious and we're pretty sure that he turned to look our way so we're pretty sure that it was Keith Morrison. So I googled and I looked around and tried to figure out why he might be in my town. Because you know, when he's around... It's like Jessica Fletcher and "Murder She Wrote". Something's going down, and it's not good. When I was a kid, my parents were very strict about TV time. We could watch "Murder She Wrote", "Barnaby Jones", "Star Trek", tennis matches and "Little House on the Prairie". Partaay! I always wished Laura Ingalls would come and be my friend and I could show her all the new technology. I would go for long walks that I called my "imagination walks" and I would dream of lots of things and one of the things I dreamed about, was being her friend. Visiting her house, her visiting mine. But that's not the point.

So I was researching Keith Morrison and I came across an interview someone did of him, talking about why he became the reporter that he did. He talked about the fact that when he was at home at one point watching TV, he saw a newscaster and he thought "I could do that". And then his career began. Something about that grabbed so tightly. "I could do that". Have you ever heard that quote by I don't know who, that goes, "if you think you can or if you think you can't... You're right " I don't know. Maybe a little hokey, but, Keith Morrison said. "I could do that." And he believed in himself, and he tried, and he was right. He could do that. And now you and I are thinking about Keith Morrison and I made that happen, so you're welcome.

And so recently, my friend Rodette, who knew from what I've shared on my social media page about my struggling with multiple sclerosis and how I'm always dropping food on the floor, which is mind blowingly annoying to say the least. So she sent me a text and told me that she was thinking about me, and that she wanted to bring dinner to my children and me. And she asked me to please say yes. Which I promptly did. Her energy was just right. And so she came over with her arms full of a main dish and a side dish and a fruit salad and bottles of water and pretzels dipped in chocolate covered sprinkles. She had made those. She recently started a business, selling her chocolates. She named the company "Lily's Sweet Shop". Lily.

When she came over, and she put the food down, she gave me a hug and looked at me and said, "I see you and I got you. I got you". She said that her grandmother had taught her that even even when you don't have money, share your food, share a meal, show your care and kindness and consideration and thoughtfulness and empathy through food. And so that's what she did for me. Let me tell you something, I like chickpeas, but I have never tasted anything as incredible as her chickpeas. I don't know what she did, but damn they were good. She told me that she was committing to bringing meals like this to me and my children twice a month every month. She asked me to please not be too proud about accepting what she was offering, because she's offering it with kindness and care and love. And I believed her.

And I asked her why she had created Lily's Sweet Shop. She gave me a lot of background and then she said that someone brought her some chocolates that they had made, and she loved them and she looked at them and thought, "I could do that." Just like Keith, I thought. "I could do that". She was right and so her company was born. She's on instagram @lily_sweet_shop.

Rodette has kept her word. She has her own life and work and children; her oldest is getting ready to head off to college. Her life is full and she always makes sure that my children and me are part of it. Her food is fantastic and the concept makes my heart sing. She saw that help was needed. She cared and she did something about it. She reminds me that I am not alone in this world. And these are things I'm grateful for. These are the people I'm grateful for. Keith Morrison. Rodette. Chickpeas. and Lily.

Chapter Thirty-Six

Therapy in a Balloon

I don't understand why therapy works. I don't really think that anything I'm saying is revolutionary or terribly enlightened. Paying somebody to listen to you at a specific time in a specific place. Paying someone to in some way, through whatever they're saying or hearing, help guide you forward. I don't get any of it.

I can theorize and hypothesize and I can certainly copy what it says in a dictionary or somewhere online. But inside of me, I really don't understand why, it works. And, for me, it does work.

I'm really thankful that I've taken the time and given that to myself. To understand so much more about myself. So much more about my choices. So very much more about my choices. And... It feels good to know why I made the choices I did; ones that I never would ever again make; those bad decisions. And it feels good to know and understand why I never would. Ever again. Make the same choices.

It's free-ing. (Is that a word?) How I see it...

So you're a little kid again at your friend's birthday party. The balloons have all been blown up with helium; not some adult just sitting there huffing and puffing, but the real deal helium stuff. I'm picturing my favorite color balloon and it's filled with helium and I'm hugging it tightly because, you know, if you let a helium balloon go, it will fly up to the sky and you're never seeing it again. And it's pretty and it's mine and I'm holding onto it tightly, so it doesn't fly away. Well, is it mine? I mean, I'm holding onto it, but is it mine? But anyway, I'm holding so tightly onto the balloon that I can't run around with everybody at the party. I can't play the games. I can't eat the cake. My arms are filled with this balloon, and I don't wanna let it go. I don't want it to fly away from me. And I see that the other kids have their balloons and they're sucking the air out of them and making their voices sound funny. So after a little bit, I decide to try too.

I hold on really tightly to my balloon...I take out some of that helium ...and I start talking. And it's hilarious. And it's weird. Everybody's doing it, but I sort of feel like they're looking strangely at me. But it was fun and the balloon isn't so full anymore. It's easier to wrap my arms around it. So I try again. And I still sound kind of weird. And I'm still uncomfortable with how people are reacting. But it's a lot easier to hold onto the balloon now. And I want to have fun at this party.

So I try again and I try again. And I try again. And it doesn't sound so funny anymore. It doesn't sound so weird anymore. I'm kind of used to it. And I really want to have some cake.

So I decide that I don't really need to hold onto it anymore. And there's still enough helium in the balloon that when I let go, it zooms around in a zigzagging, non-direction, before seemingly giving up and collapsing to the ground. It's empty. Cause I let it go. And I can talk just fine without it. I don't need to hold onto that balloon. I don't think it was all mine anyway. I'm just a little kid at a birthday party. I'm going to have some cake.

CHAPTER THIRTY-SEVEN

There is no magic and this won't help

I have held several free networking events in my town. Because of my social media page, I know so many people and businesses and organizations, and I support them all. I know so many people who I think would benefit from knowing other people. I know businesses whose locations aren't in high foot traffic areas and could use more attention. I know when there are specials and sales and charitable organizations that could use some volunteers. I see it all from my vantage point and I can see it all, almost no matter how I'm physically feeling. I can still look and connect and help, even on days when walking just takes more effort than I can give it. Or my hand hurts too much or my body is too dizzy. I can still sit in my chair or lay on the floor, if that's where I've landed for the moment, and I can connect and help others. I guess the internet isn't all bad.

These networking events I've held are an opportunity for me to bring all of this information and all of these people together. They've been incredibly successful and I'm really proud of what I've done. Businesses have benefited time and again, because of me. That feels wonderful. The last one I held at The Gravity Vault on Seymour, was difficult for me because so much was happening in terms of multiple sclerosis and my health. I was experiencing some setbacks that weighed very heavily on my heart and mind. I could not put as much into it as I usually had and I decided to take a break on holding those events because of it.

So many incredible people came to each one of my events. We had one at The Fit Loft on Erie and Wine & Design on Glenridge and The Montclair Brewery on Walnut. Walnut Street, where the festival was when I got lost. Right near Ray's Luncheonette and Walnut Street Kitchen; they've been doing Dim Sum on Sundays and I really want to try. And Brick & Dough, their Brussels sprouts are insane. What else? Montclair Baby! I saw that they had a hypnobirthing class there. I did that with my son! I felt ZERO pain for my second birth and he was born in 6 minutes. He was born as I laughed at something I found absurd and laughed so hard that my laughter, laughed him into the world. As my doctor said, "Your laughter is bringing your son to you!". My Yithak Shaysh. Oh! The Montclair Township Animal Shelter is right there; so many volunteers from there have come to my events. I love having them speak and their passion for helping animals is immense.

One woman came with her wonderful wife and I just found out that they're pregnant! It's a girl and I have a little present but shhhh, it's a surprise. She thanked me for allowing her to speak at my events, even though she doesn't have a business. But wow, of course I wanted her to speak. Volunteers at animal shelters are making it a part of their lives, to speak for those who cannot speak for themselves. So speak on my friends, speak on. Oh and The Windough! You have got to try it- only Saturday mornings, and only from 8 until they sell out, which can be 9:30! Oh my goodness and Egans and Halcyon and there's an Incredible Thai place there that starts with S and I can't remember the name. Sukhumvit. I looked it up. And there's more and I have to stop because I've clearly segued into my @WeAreMontclair mode. I need to focus.

I'm on Fire Island and we're heading to the beach as soon as I'm done with this chapter. We're renting a house in Ocean Beach and I love it so much. I'd love to have a house here of my own and I'd escape all of the time. A house with a pool. In Seaview? Ocean Bay Park? The air is just better here for me.

Would I want a house on the Bay and we'd watch the sunsets each night or on the beach and we'd watch the sun rise? Or a house with a huge deck on top, so I could always see both. Yeah, that's it. I taught my kids how to tell directions here with one of my kiddo-creations: "WEST is the sunset, so that is the Bay. That's how we know, it's the end of the day. EAST is the sunrise, so that is the beach. Sunscreen and water and towels for each. And now we have WE, yes NOW, we have WE!! And once we have WE, it's easy to see!! Exactly where NORTH and SOUTH should be." I call it "we have WE". Of course. I think Kwame Alexander would be impressed with that one. I met him at the Montclair Literary Festival. I'm going to put a picture of the two of us, somewhere in this book. I wonder where it will flow the best? I am loving writing this book you guys. I've never done anything like this and I'm loving every single thing about it. I am a writer.

And back to my Fire Island. We don't use our phones out here for directions or for much at all really. I love it here and this is my happiest of happy places. I love being by the water, it makes me feel free. And next happiest is Christiansted. Or Frederiksted actually. Then Edipsos. Then NYC. Then La Jolla. Then Venice. Then Aruba. Then Asbury Park. Then Cape May. Then... hmmmm...I'm not sure of the order and once again... Focus!

And I'd like to have a house in all of those places or just 5 of them. Or just 2 of them. No. All of them. An apartment or condo would be fine in some and on the beach in the others and a pool and I'd like to bring our dog Schemmy whenever possible. The last dogs I had before I had children were Emily and Schatzi. I would call Emily "Emmy-Pemmy". And I would call Schatzi, Governor Pataki. And the nickname for that was "Governor", of course, but with the accent and tone of a British Butler. Of course. Think Tim Curry in "Clue". Got it? And sometimes I'd actually call her Schatzi too. But that's a long story. It's actually not a long story and it involves my little brother, but I'm pretty sure that that's not the point of this chapter. Oh wait, but I was telling you something. Oh yeah, so I really broke down when they died, and I had decided that I would not get any more dogs ever again. And then I had kids and they convinced me otherwise. The final convincing was when they picked out the name. They suggested we use both Schatzi and Emmy. They named her Schemmy. And she can tell I'm unstable before I can, and she warns us. And if I've already fallen, she won't leave my side, no matter what. Not even for a T-R-E-A-T. And I'm glad that I have her and we love her very much and I've taught her sign language. I wrote and narrated an incredible short story inspired by her. It's called "She's such a good girl" and it's great. If you like dogs, you'll like it. Damn, I've said too much. And so my networking events, that's where we were.

I've met so many wonderful people and I wish I could mention them all. I met one woman who came to all of my events with her husband, who is great too, and they are delicious together. They remind me of Dagmara and Patrick, and Kevin and Kyra, and Dan & Day; their place @dananddays_ is on Valley & Bellevue & it's so good! I love their strawberry lemonade. Ahhhh! I can't stop!! Ok, so my events!

I met so many people at my events and I'm sure that one of you is reading this now. So if it's one of you, HIIII!! I'm writing this chapter while wearing my We Are Montclair shirt, jeans shorts and of course, my boots. I'm in character, can you see me? Thanks for reading this. I appreciate it. So the woman I met, she's a doctor and she has a business that is based in alternative and holistic health. She's on Park Street. She impressed me, her husband impressed me and he runs his own incredible business too. I went to her site and I read about her treatment options and I scheduled a call with her. We talked for a while. I spoke to her specifically about the pop rocks and tingling sensations in my foot and toes and leg. I wondered if something specific she did would be helpful. It was clear to me from what I read and heard, that one treatment of hers was in fact very helpful to very many. I'm an advertising lawyer, I know truth when I see it. And I wondered if that treatment would help with this.

And there's another doctor in town I know, who has been here for a really long time. He's on Park Street too. We went to him when we needed a chiropractor for as long as I can remember. When we were little and my younger sister, the ballerina, hurt her ankle, he was the one we went to. He fixed her. When my dad had back problems, he went there and felt so much better. When I was pregnant with my son and my hip was displaced, and I was in a lot of pain, I walked into his office, balanced by a cane. Acupuncture, and my pain was gone, my cane wasn't needed and I walked out feeling really good. He was a nice guy, he is a nice guy. A smart guy and also, as far as I was concerned, he was basically, a magician. His office was always busy and there was never a long wait. And when he'd come into the examining room, he would say hello and he would talk to you like you were a human being, looking for his help. You know, like a doctor. He always wanted to help.

He always answered my questions. He would never make me feel like I was rushed or, taking too much of his time. He would always calmly, patiently, kindly answer my questions. I told him once that I really appreciated his intelligence and demeanor and his care and his kindness. He told me that when he was first starting out as a doctor, he got an eye exam from my dad. He said that he was so impressed

with my dad's intelligence and demeanor and care and kindness. He told me that in large part, he modeled the way he treats his patients after the way my dad treated his. I'm proud of my dad. And when no one else had any other suggestions about the pop rocks and pins and needles in my foot and my leg, I went to him. I told him I needed some magic. I couldn't think of anybody else who had any.

She told me that while that treatment is very helpful for very many, she did not believe that it would help me. She would love to try other treatments to help other issues and for this specific problem, this would not help.

He told me that he would love to try other treatments to help other issues. And I knew for sure that he could help with those. And for this specific problem, he told me that there is no magic.

They were patient and kind and they answered my questions. They weren't defensive and their egos did not get in the way. They did not make it about them or their lives or their stories. They listened to me. They listened to me. They talked to me like I was a human being, looking for help. You know, like a doctor. They both wanted to help me. In many ways they did.

Dr. Ashley Twynam from Earthly Living and Dr Peter Haigney.

There is no magic and this won't help.

Those were the best doctor appointments I've had in a really long time.

We Are Montclair

thisisagreatidea.etsy.com

CHAPTER THIRTY-EIGHT

I didn't even know what day it was

So do you know the singer Laufey? My kids love her music and shared her music with me and I fell in love with it too. Her singing reminds me a lot of one of my absolute musical heroes Norah Jones. One of my favorite songs by Norah Jones is "Come Away With Me". I've loved that song since it came out during my law school days; sometimes we'd take breaks from studying to dance and this was one of our favorite songs of escape. But that's not the point.

My kids love Laufey so much and as a present for my son's Bar Mitzvah, I got us incredible tickets to go see her at Radio City Music Hall. Incredible tickets. Like, way out of my price range at Radio City, incredible. And it was worth every single penny. I took so much video that evening of my kids singing her songs with her only feet away from them. Her music was so beautiful and I loved hearing her, but watching my kids hearing her was absolute magic. Watching my kids feeling the joy of that moment. Pretty much the whole night is of me videotaping my kids, watching her sing. It was magic.

At one point in the evening, she announced that she was bringing one of her heroes on stage to sing with her. And she welcomed to the stage... Norah Jones. Norah. Jones. My musical hero. Norah Jones got on stage and sang my favorite song of hers, "Come Away With Me" with Laufey. And I cried. It was one of the best nights of my life. I just kept saying "I don't believe it. I don't believe it." I was like a cartoon character in a movie, clutching my head and shaking it back-and-forth and back-and-forth. I couldn't believe it. I purchased these tickets for the joy my children would feel, which brings me so much joy and these tickets brought me one of my heroes, singing one of my favorite songs. The night was absolute magic.

We took the train into NYC which was fun and we hadn't done that in a while. The bus line that used to run through my town, the DeCamp bus line, doesn't run there anymore so the train is pretty much the only option. There is this relatively new place called BoxCar, I should look into to see if it's another good option. But, that's not the point.

We walked from Penn over to Radio City. Just before we crossed the street to go to the concert my daughter and I both changed our shoes. She changed to her cute ballet flats and I changed to my hot pink red bottom Louboutin boots. Any excuse to wear those babies. They may be rain boots, but it does not have to be raining for me to wear them. It's actually kind of nice because when I go out wearing those boots, they're definitely eye-catching, and so many women have made a point of coming over to me to say that they like my boots. Like a connection with strangers for no reason other than my hot pink red bottom Louboutin boots. I think that's really cool. I like saying nice things to people and of course I like it when I get that from others too. You know? When somebody sees something nice about you and then thinks something nice about you and then feels something nice about you and then decides to say it. They decide to say that thing, that they thought, that they felt, that they saw. They decided to say that nice thing. That's a lot of steps to kindness and I appreciate all of them. But that's not the point.

After the concert, we decided we were going to head to a diner, but then we were all really tired so I decided we were gonna go wild and crazy and actually splurge to get an Uber home. But we all had to go to the bathroom. And we had already exited Radio City so we couldn't go back in to go to the bathroom. So we started walking. And walking. And walking... It was so weird. Every single place we went to in New York City was closed! I didn't understand it! Finally, we got to restaurant/club which was clearly for adults and there was a really tall big bouncer out front. He was a very serious bouncer. And he was not moving from his spot. I walked up to him and asked if he would please help. That my kid needed to go to the bathroom and we'd walked and every place was closed and my kid really needed to go to the bathroom; we're not gonna stay… He looked at my kids and said ok, so that was handled.

So we ordered the Uber and it was gonna arrive in a few minutes and the bouncer said, "You know there's a speakeasy next-door?" I didn't. He pointed towards what looked like a pretty empty-looking, sterile -looking vestibule area with a plain old desk and a woman sitting behind it. And he said it was really cool in there and that we should check it out. So I wrote down the name and thought that, OK, someday I will. I thanked him and he said that he thought I should go check it out now. I told him our Uber was coming and that I was with kids, so probably not? And he told me not to worry about it. So he brought my kids and me into this vestibule with this woman at this desk. She looked at us and looked at him questioningly. He told her that he wanted us to check it out, that we're friends of his and he wanted us to see the place. So she said sure. And she took us down a hallway to a stairwell that looked really long and dark and ominous. And I thought… This is New York. And I was loving the fact that my kids were getting this New York experience.

So we went down the sterile staircase with a few people coming up and looking questioningly at this woman with her children. And of course, checking out my amazing boots. And we went down into this hallway and she opened the doors into a magical Wonderland. It was a Speakeasy. There was jazz playing, there were people talking, laughing, dancing. The bar was this rich mahogany. We were, by the opening of those doors, transported into another time and place. It felt like a wonderland and I loved it immediately. That bouncer, who wasn't moving from his spot, except for to bring us to this woman, was exactly right. It was perfect. I'd love to find it and go back there some day. We looked around and smiled with gratitude and headed back up to meet our Uber driver. I wanted to say thank you to our bouncer friend, but he was gone. No trace of him. He made the end of our night in New York City absolutely perfect, and then "poof" he was gone. And if he's reading this, thanks man. But that's not the whole point.

The point is that this wonderful, magical, dream, fulfilling, musical, other worldly experience of a day and night... It was May 3. My day of freedom, that means so much to me. And, for the first time since that mint lemonade on Church Street, I didn't even realize that it was May 3. Some time has passed, and that day, that I think the universe is always going to be make a magical one for me, didn't fill me with the awareness of what the next day was and had been. I told my kids I got tickets to see Laufey on May 3. And my son asked me if I got the tickets for that day specifically to help me through that difficult day. And I had no idea what he was talking about. Some time has passed. May 3 and Laufey. It was perfect. And I didn't even know what day it was.

My loves

CHAPTER THIRTY-NINE

The ones who didn't make it

S everal times now, I believed that I was done writing this book. I felt like I had said what I needed to say, and was ready to wrap it up and publish it. And then I'd think of something else that I wanted to add. Or a correction I wanted to make. Or I'd think of a chapter that absolutely had to be included, like the quicksand chapter that I just thought of the other day while I was talking to someone, trying to explain how stuck this disease makes me feel. And then I add more and more and the book isn't finished.

I reached out to my friend Kate, who wrote an incredible book, "Transister". Her book really moved me and grabbed me and it was written so beautifully. She put in a portion relating her life and her feelings to Genesis in the Bible. It was so clever and insightful and I didn't want it to end! You got to read it; really good. I reached out to her to ask her if she went through this as well. The feeling that you're not really sure when you're done. And also, the feeling that I wrote a lot of chapters that were really really good and they just don't go with the flow of this book. And I wonder, "what do I do with those chapters"? Do I write some short stories? Do I make YouTube videos of me reciting them? They're really good chapters. Some about a woman named Lindsay who I worked with at a firm New York City. She's an incredible author, too, I could reach out to her as well for her thoughts. She wrote, "Big Law" and "No one needs to know" and "Just one Look". I love of her books. They're the perfect, summer chill at home or beach books.

I wrote chapters about lots of other women who impress me like Lindsay and Kate and a woman named Victoria who wrote a book called "The Power of Justice"; which is a must read about our justice system. I wrote about a woman I know named Amanda who created a business that caters to and provides space and inspiration for other creative people. I wrote about a woman named Rose, who my kids call Grandma; about women named Cynthia, Francesca, Tasha, the Ashleys and the Jessicas. I wrote what could have been a book, about Maureen and Karen. I have so much to say about Maureen and Karen. I wrote about Danielle and Nancy and so many more. I wrote a lot of good stuff and I don't know what to do with it, but it doesn't really fit in the flow of this book.

So I'll put it away for now and focus on wrapping up and publishing this book. My printer just broke. Someday, I'll have a big high-speed printer. Color and black and white. One side or both sides printing options. I don't need it to be a scanner or a fax machine or a BMI calculator. I'd just like a really good, extra ink included, highspeed printer. But that's not the point.

I guess maybe the point I'm coming to is that I'll write another book at some point. And I'll compile the chapters that didn't flow in this one. And if I do, I hope you'll read that too. Maybe the title of this chapter should be the title of that book. Something like, "women who impress me" or, "the lost chapters" or, "The ones who didn't make it". I don't know. For now, I want to get to what's next. Before I move to what's next though, I want to talk about just one of those women.

Chapter Forty

You get 2 ounces

So I went to this one doctor soon after I was diagnosed and I told him about this medicine that I heard about. I told him that I had heard and read that some people with multiple sclerosis could benefit from this medicine. I told him that I'd never used this type of medicine before and I didn't know anything about it, but I really wanted to try. I never would've wanted to try it before but it's supposed to help people with multiple sclerosis so I asked him if I could get it. He said sure. I'll give you a prescription. And I had to fill out all these things and the prescription he handed me, it turns out was for 2 ounces. So I asked him where the pharmacy was but he didn't know, so I googled it, and I found a few pharmacies near me that I could go to.

So I went into the pharmacy and I looked all around at all the medication and I asked them to give me 2 ounces. And they asked me what kind and I told him I didn't know. I just wanted 2 ounces. And they said ok but there were all types of different medicine here at that pharmacy. There were pills and there were liquids and there were things where you have to put a drop under your tongue and there were ones that had different flavors and there were ones that do these things and ones that do those things... Which ones do I want? Just give me 2 ounces. Mix it up I guess? I have multiple sclerosis and I've heard that this type of medicine can help. I don't know what kind. I don't really know what it does. But my doctor gave me a prescription. For 2 ounces. I can get 2 ounces. So they gave me a random 2 ounces of different types of medicine in their pharmacy.

And I didn't know what it was for exactly, and I didn't know how to ingest it, and I didn't know how it would make me feel and I didn't know what it would do. Because I didn't have any guidance.

Have you ever gone to see a doctor because you're sick and have them tell you to go and find a Pharmacy because they don't know where the pharmacies are? Have you ever gone to go see a doctor because you're sick and have them tell you they'll write you a prescription for medicine, but they won't tell you what kind? Have you ever gone into a pharmacy with a prescription, the only detail being how many ounces of medicine you get? A "you pick!" kind of deal? And they just give you a whole bunch of random things without any guidance or instruction? Without any clue as to what it will do? If it's actually going to help you with anything that you need help with? Sounds pretty damn crazy doesn't it.

Nothing about this disease makes any damn sense.

I found a dispensary in Bloomfield, New Jersey, called Blue Oak NJ. It's run by a woman who understands this struggle and wanted to make it easier. And she made it so much easier. She made it easier with the products she carries and she made it easier with the people she hired. They know what they're talking about and they want to help. They've helped. She's made it so much easier for me. I don't know what's next but I know that I want to thank you, Danielle.

CHAPTER FORTY-ONE

I don't know

At the end of last year, not really New Year's resolution but around New Year's resolution time, I decided that I wanted a few things and that a few things were going to happen for me. Like the concept of manifesting, you know? I decided/manifested/thought of/dreamed of Number One, having a lot of money. I took a page out of Jim Carrey's book and I wrote myself a check for $550,000 for my birthday this year. And I'm going to cash that check. And I've decided I will still have $650,000 in my bank account. Next year there will be more. I wrote it all out. It wasn't a vision board, but you know what I'm talking about if I say vision board. I wrote down how much money this year and how much money next year and I kept saying $550,000 for this year. But my mind kept saying no, $650,000. Every time I thought 550, my mind said no, 650. So I decided, I'll write the check for 550 and I'll still have 650. Boom.

And I sent an email to a few people that my best friend Andrea found online who are connected with Beaches Turks and Caicos, and told them how much I loved it there. I told them about the last vacation that I had there when I thought I was going to die. I told them that since then, I'd been diagnosed with MS and I can't work anymore and I have disability money, which is so much better than nothing, but also about half of the money that I used to bring in. I don't have the money to go to Beaches Turks and Caicos anymore. The Italian Village with the bunkbeds and video games and butler service. I thought we'd go back. I'd love to go back. I want to go back there knowing that yes, I have multiple sclerosis and no, this is Not our last vacation together. I hope someone gets back to me. I want to go back there with my babies, who I suppose now are no longer babies, but will always be my babies. That's the second thing I want.

So we've got the 550 and the remaining 650, Jim Carrey style. We've got the Beaches, Turks and Caicos, Italian Village family suite with bunkbeds and butler service.

And I want to walk in a fashion show. That's the third thing that I want. I want to walk in a fashion show, I always wanted to be a model, an actress, a performer... I mean, I was on the Guiding Light! We can leave out the fact that it was only a few seconds and I didn't have any lines. Cause that's not the point.

I want to be a runway model wearing my signature hot-pink-red-bottom-Louboutin boots. They are bad-ass. They're chunky heels so they're not hard to walk in. Even when my balance isn't so great, I can still walk in them. They're actually very comfortable. I wear them with shorts, skirts, jeans... Anytime I'd run a networking event, I'd wear them. There's this place in town, it's a paint and sip place called "Wine and Design" on Glenridge Ave. and Rachel, the woman who runs it, was inspired by the fact that I had to learn how to walk again. I've had to learn how to walk again twice since I was diagnosed. She was so inspired by that, and inspired by my dog who can sense when I'm getting sick before I can, so she held an event at her place inspired by me. The theme of the event was, "It's a good day for a walk". And the picture that everybody there painted was someone walking across a crosswalk, wearing boots, walking their dog. People painted whatever color boots they wanted; of course mine were pink. Several of them did the hot pink for me and my boots. Everybody did whatever kind of dog they wanted to do; they have incredible artist art-instructors there. And 40% of the proceeds from the event, went to Paws Animal Shelter, which is just incredible. I never would have imagined that something so good could happen for others as a result of my having to learn to walk again. Money was donated to help shelter animals, because of me and my struggles and my determination. I am grateful for that. What a beautiful thing. But that's not the point.

The point is that on top of the 550, 650, Beaches Turks and Caicos, I want to walk in fashion shows. And I want to get paid for it. There's so much that's out of my control and yes, yes, money can't buy everything and money can't buy happiness...but in my heart and in my soul, I am happy. I don't need money for that. But the comfort of knowing that my bills are paid, that I would love. And because cleaning is so difficult, I could hire somebody to clean sometimes. Because cooking can be difficult, I could hire somebody to cook sometimes. I'd love to be one of those people who could do that. I'd like to be one of those people who could put another bathroom in next to my bedroom, an en-suite kind of thing you know? I'd like to be one of those people who could upgrade their early 1900's bathroom and make it nicer and more friendly for me on shaky days when I need a more friendly kind of bathroom. I'd like to be one of those people who had a bathroom on every single floor of the house. I'd like to be one of those people who could have a pool like I did when I was a kid.

I had money twice. As a child we had money and that disappeared with the divorce. As an adult, I had money as a lawyer and that disappeared with the disease. I worked very hard to become a lawyer. About 5% of lawyers in America are black. An even smaller percentage of them are women. I worked very hard to finish college and to buy my house and to have my kids and to become a lawyer. And I will never practice as a lawyer again. I worked so hard to climb back up from the destruction from that divorce-collapse of life. I didn't see the MS collapse coming. I was not prepared for all of the destruction it would bring.

I was about to write that I'll never make the kind of money again like I did when I was a practicing attorney, but that's fine. Because I don't want to make that kind of money again. I want to make more. But that's not the point.

The point is that we have 550, 650, Turks and Caicos, the cooking and cleaning, and walking in a runway. I believe all of these things will happen. Jim Carrey style I'm cashing that check for $550,000 on my birthday. I'm doing it. It's on my fireplace mantle and I look at it every day. I'm cashing that check. And also, I was just in touch with a woman who follows me on my social media page, and who put me in touch with her doctor's office. She told me that the MS patients there walk in a fashion show. When she told me that, I smiled. Maybe I'll walk in that fashion show too.

I am a survivor. I won't give up no matter what the odds are against me. I won't give up no matter how I am treated or mistreated. I won't give up because people don't speak my language. I won't give up in spite of the pain and exhaustion and dizziness and confusion. I won't give up and I won't back down because that is who I am. In spite of the hard days. In spite of the frustration. I am thankful that I am who I am in spite of, not because of, multiple sclerosis. I am grateful for so much. And also, I will not ever believe that all of this has happened for a reason and I will never be grateful for so much. And that's ok. I'm on my way to figuring out my best life and aside from the set backs, all in all, I'm enjoying the ride. I have my children and our home filled with love and we are happy. I don't know what today, tomorrow, or the next day will bring with multiple sclerosis. I don't know.

But what I do know is coming: 550. 650. Beaches T&C. And me. A fashion model. Wearing my signature hot-pink-red-bottom-Louboutin boots.
It's going to happen. It's a done deal. It just hasn't happened yet. For these things. For so many things. I am grateful. I think that's the point.

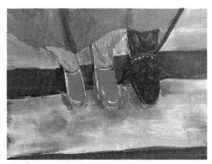

Andrea's painting.

My other loves

"I gotta be me."

Credit MHS Yearbook Staff

Chapter Forty-Two

It tastes like fear and it's easier with the shirt

As I look through my phone, adding some pictures as my final touches to wrap up this book, I'm having a hard time choosing what to include. I think I'm just about done writing. I'm self-publishing this and I'm so excited. I'll make something like $2 for every book sold, but I don't care. I'm so excited to share this. I like this book a lot and I'm proud of myself for writing it. I think I'll upload it on Amazon? I know my friends around town will have book reading/signing events for me at their stores and restaurants. I'm excited to figure that out. I know people who are with me on my "We Are Montclair" page, will be supportive of this book. I hope you'll check out the businesses I've mentioned. I wonder if they'll get some business from this. I hope so. I hope you'll buy the books that I mentioned, that my friends wrote. They're impressive women. You should check them out.

I've been using a site called Atticus to write and format this. Formatting has been really difficult and I've gone through a lot of revisions. But customer support has been helpful. I don't have a publisher and I wouldn't know how to go about getting one. I think I have to buy an ISBN number. I'll do that before

I upload it. I've done my best at editing and formatting, so if you see an error, please be gentle. And if you know me, just let me know. Cool thing about this digital self-publishing is that I can edit it if I want to. I like that. I won't change content but I wouldn't mind hearing if there's a typo or something.

I wrote a really good children's book after my daughter was born. I've recently updated it; some of the words and all of the pictures. My daughter has a friend who is a really gifted artist, so I hired her to do all of the illustrations. The book is now magnificent. And the library in town contacted me to be a guest reader in the town's "Big Read" event. And they said I can read the book! I love reading children's books, so I'd do it anyway but how cool that I'll get to share my book. Share the activity that goes with my book. I'm really excited. I'm going to get to read in the Big Read Chair! I'm so thankful for it all. I hope you'll read that too. It's for adults as well. My kids helped me with the final flow of the updated book. I'll self publish that next.

When it comes to this book, my kids have both read through it and have really helped. They've given me their thoughts, notes and corrections. Their help has been invaluable. The flow of the book works better now that my Editors-in-Chief, have worked their magic. It has been important for us to read and absorb all of this as a family. They knew most and have learned some. They've asked questions and I've answered everything to the best of my ability. We've talked a lot about it all. We always talk a lot. About everything. We're not discouraged by discomfort. I'm thankful for that. I'm thankful for us. Writing this book has been really good for us. I appreciate these two so, so much.

And also, I'm feeling pretty strongly that you may not be grasping the magnitude of what happened in this picture.

Exhibit A) LOOK. AT. OUR.
HANDS.

So here's what happened. I saw Bryan Cranston on stage in "Network".
Holy hell. Loved. Then I waited by the back door of the theater, with a bunch of
other crazy stalkers. And he came out of the door and he had a Massive Serious
Bodyguard, who was not tryin to smile, a drink in hand and a total famous
person car waiting for him. He was so freaking cool. He looked like a movie.
And it was his Birthday! And someone there already knew it was his birthday
and came prepared with a birthday gift. That's next level. I did not know it
was his birthday. Do famous people open gifts from fans? I would absolutely,
unequivocally, hell-to-the-no, not. Hell no. People are nuts. Maybe a court jester
or taster or someone else could open them. That sounds elitist and insensitive
and I'd probably want that. Did you ever see "The Court Jester" with Danny
Kaye? Incredible. I could watch that a million times. And "Singing in the Rain"
too. That might be my favorite movie. Anyway, it was Bryan's birthday. I can
refer to him as just "Bryan" because we've held hands. See exhibit A.

So it was my drinking buddy Bryan C's birthday and if you know me, you know, I. Love. Birthdays. I love them. I have thrown some Amazing parties for my kids. Ok, I'm listening to music and I'm clearly on the, yup. I'm on a "Favorite Songs of The Muppets" soundtrack on Spotify. That "Mah Na Mah Na" song I danced to with my kids a few days ago is sending me on a musical journey that may not be quite right for me at this time. It's a lot. Hang on. OK, wait, this song is fun. "Mr. Bassman" by the Little Apple Band. It's reminding me of Grease. I know just about every line to that movie. I loved Grease 2 also. And? Challenge me on that, you won't win. My little sister and I would pretend we were Pink Ladies. I was for Halloween last year. The boots sealed the deal. You know, my hot pink red bottom Christian Louboutin boots. Have I mentioned those? I bought them for myself when I learned how to walk again. For the second time. Those boots were because I could walk again. I feel proud of myself when I wear those boots. Have I mentioned the boots? And I had a crush on Maxwell Caulfield, but who didn't. I was a member of the Sean Cassidy Fan Club. I still have my jacket. I loved Saturday Night Fever too. Well, all things John Travolta. My mom and I used to Strut sometimes when we went out. I'd always imagine The Bee Gees were there singing with us. Can you say non-sequitur. I always have a lot on my mind.

But so back to my life-long friend, Bryan. How cool to be acting on Broadway on your birthday! And to come outside to a bunch of people who adore you, and applaud when you appear. I mean, that's got to feel unbelievable. On one of my birthdays, I walked over to Broadway, the street, and I sang. So technically, I sang on Broadway on that birthday. One birthday, Lizzie and I went to see "War Horse", which was so depressing, and someone I knew worked backstage, so we got to go on stage and I sang and danced. So technically, I sang and danced on Broadway for that birthday. At the last networking event I held in my town, I thanked everyone for being there. Then a woman named Wendy, said that they all wanted to thank me for all I've done for them and for our community. They all clapped for me. And they were all already standing. So technically, I got a standing ovation at that event. I think everyone should get a standing ovation at least once in their lives. So what I'm saying, is that my best friend Bryan and I, totally get each other. Shared life experiences and all.

And also, Look. At. Our. Hands!!
You can't miss it. It's clear as day. And, so, I went to take a picture with him and just like that, I suddenly became unable to figure out how words work. I managed to come up with, "EVERYTHING I'VE SEEN YOU DO IS GREAT!!" Whatever. I give that an A for effort. He laughed a kind laugh and said, "Well, I doubt that, but I appreciate it anyway". It made me like him more. He was nice.

And also, I was on a date, and I had completely forgotten that I was on a date. I was blinded by Bryan like any totally stable, non-stalker-like- admirer, would be. And suddenly I remembered that oh yeah, I'm here with someone. And I looked around for him; he was sort of hopping up and down behind Bryan. I felt a little badly and I also thought it was really funny. So I said, "oh right. Honey! Come meet Bryan". And I waved him over, so he would stop with the hopping, and also so he could have his turn with fame. And then Bryan Cranston started laughing!! He said, "OH! Yes! Honey!!! You're still here?!?! Would you come take a picture honey! Come here honey!!" I. Fucking. Plotzed. Bryan Cranston was doing improv with me. Yes he was. Don't take this from me. He was riffing with me! He thought I was funny! Bryan Cranston was laughing because of something I said! Are. You. KIDDING. ME !?!? I mean, STOP IT! That! Happened.

And so to keep the connection going, I said something really clever like, "I like pink" or "I met Molly Ringwald!" I don't know. What I said during those precious moments with my dearest friend Bryan, is not what matters. What does matter is that he was kind to me. He was kind to all of us crazy stalker people standing by a back door on a cold New York City night. And we all sang Happy Birthday to him. And it was nice to be a part of a group of people who were making a point to be nice to a stranger. He's famous and all but he's also just another person who had a birthday and we all were there singing to him. It made everyone feel good. I was thankful to be a part of that. And I was so thankful that Bryan Cranston believed that I should star in an upcoming movie with him. And that Bryan Cranston thought I should be one of his new, Highly-paid writers! That he thinks someday I'll host Saturday Night Live?! What?!?!?! I mean, I think that too!! But, Bryan Cranston thinks that?!?! What- you didn't sense he felt that way?? Well. I did. He does. Do NOT take this away from me.

And I wish I could have told her about it all. Every second. I wish she could read this. She would've loved this chapter.

Cause Lizzie and I used to watch Breaking Bad together. Well, not physically together cause she was in New York and I was in New Jersey. But we'd call each other and sit on the phone together for the entire episode. We wouldn't even speak, but we were watching it together and we knew we were both there. She could handle scarier things better than I could, so it felt good to have her company. When we couldn't talk during the show, we'd steadily text and when there were commercials, we'd text like crazy about what just happened. There were commercials back then, right? That's how I remember it. AMC? We loved watching it and catching up after to talk about it. All week long, we'd text each other with predictions and "do you believe that happened??!?!", discussions. When I met him, I wished she was around. I wished I could call her and tell her, "I met Bryan Cranston from Breaking Bad!". We would have been screaming on the phone about it! I would have given her a second by second run down of it all. He was wearing a black leather coat, I think? She would've wanted to know every detail.

Drink in hand?! What was he drinking? She'd want to know. Some kind of grown up person drink; like bourbon or whiskey or scotch? I don't know drinks and one of those might be the same as the other. But one of those movie adult-drinks, where there's not much in the glass. The liquid is either clear or pancake-syrup-brown. And they never seem to drink much of it. Like, it seems like a ridiculously small amount of liquid. But everybody is always ok with paying money for such a small amount of liquid, when it comes to those types of drinks. And then they take what seems to be the tiniest of little sips and then they purse or lightly smack their lips and go, "ahhhhhhh, that's good" or "ohhhhhh!!" as they pound the bar slowly a couple of times and shake their heads; while blowing out that fire that they just swallowed. OR! they toss it back like a shot, and again, there's like a thimble's worth of liquid in that cup. But they toss it back and let us all know that this is PAINFUL for them. It Burns!! They have to open their mouths and eyes really wide and act like their tongue and their chest is on fire. And they shake their head in disbelief. Or they wipe their, not remotely wet mouth, with the back of their arm. Have you noticed actors are always heavy on the mouth wiping when there's a napkin anywhere near them in a food scene? They almost never eat. I understand that cause scenes can take long and they don't want to keep eating or it's not real food or they don't want to replace the food or whatever. But it's distracting cause the food doesn't disappear and they put like a pea on their fork if they bother. And then they chew the pea for the entire scene; distracting. But they are always wiping their mouths with their napkins. And aggressively wiping their hands with said napkin as well. Look when you're watching scenes with food, you'll see it now. I'm all about a napkin but what's with the OCD wiping of the mouth and hands? No one gets that dirty when they eat. And we can all see that they're not really eating. Is it because they need to have something to do with their hands? Does the director tell them to do that? I don't think they should. It's distracting. It takes away from the real-ness of the scene. Cause it's not real and cause just about everyone does it. Watch. You'll notice it now. You're welcome.

So after the swallowing of the liquid, there has to be a marked pause in the conversation for them to have the floor to say, "Bartender! Get me another!" And the people nearby either look shocked at this atypical, drunken, potentially foreboding behavior. Or, they look like they're thinking: Yup. Consistent behavior. That's how he rolls. And if I'm watching, the actor better actually take a sip, because I notice.

I notice when sips aren't taken, when that cheeseburger was half eaten in the last scene, but now there's only one bite missing. I notice when her hair was parted on the left when she started the sentence and she hasn't moved, but now it's parted on the right. I notice which hand people write with and if that changes, there really should be a character backstory that tells us why. Have you noticed that a lot of famous people write with their left hands? Keep an eye out now, you'll see. My kids think movie directors should hire me to watch and spot those inconsistencies. It happens a lot. I wonder why there isn't someone to check for that more often. I'm always pausing something to say to my kids, "watch her hand!" Or "look at that drink!" And then they see it too. I mean actors, directors, just put some water in that to-go coffee cup. It has a lid on it. So you'll have a cold beverage in there and then you can actually take a sip and not pretend to take a sip. It's really very distracting when those coffee cups are empty. Some might call it OCD. I call it attention to detail. I'm pretty incredible that way. I can also always tell when someone has recently gotten a haircut. Even if I haven't seen them in years. Seriously. That's weird. I know. But it's true. It's my superpower, don't knock it.

So back to the drink. When the person asks the bartender for that next drink, you look at the screen and you have to wonder why, because the experience was clearly very unpleasant. I mean, the typical and reliable actor response, was that it shocked them and it burned. Dude! Why are you asking for more? So, in sum, that was the kind of drink Bryan Cranston had in his hand that night. The vodka, tequila, brandy, scotch, bourbon, type of drink. Say Bryan Cranston five times fast. It's not hard. I just wanted you to do it. And now I wonder if you did it. Lizzie would have flipped out when I met Bryan Cranston. I wanted to tell her so badly.

I have a t-shirt that has a periodic table on it and in the table is written, "I am the one who knocks". I have another one that says it without the periodic table. Lizzie loved those shirts and got a few things for herself with that saying too. I wear one of those shirts every 6 months. I have to get MRIs twice a year now and those machines knock so loudly. I never used to be claustrophobic, but so much time in those tubes has changed that. It feels like I'm in a coffin. And they're so loud. The technicians play music but the knocking is too loud to hear it well. They give you earplugs sometimes, but it doesn't help at all. That knocking. That knocking is so loud. And it feels like I'm in a coffin every time. It feels like I'm being eased into a coffin. Don't move. Don't move. Don't breathe too deeply. Don't have an itch on your nose. Breathe shallow breaths. You can take a deep breath when you get out. It's only an hour. You can lay still in this coffin and not breath deeply, for an hour. They need a clear picture of your brain. They need a clear picture of your spine. You can't move. They're looking for more damage. You breathed too deeply, they have to start again. Don't move. Please don't move so this can end.

Fingers crossed for no more damage. The taste of saline in your mouth is fading. I always forget that's going to happen. When the needle goes in my arm it happens. I wish they'd warn me about the taste. I always forget that part. Every 6 months. It surprises me every time. Saline is the taste of my fear. They pump the taste of my fear through my veins. It surprises me every time I taste it in my mouth. Every 6 months. That knocking, it's so loud. It used to be easy to take blood from my arm, but my veins aren't so easy after all of these years of needles. I hate it all. Every time I hate it and it makes me cry and I hate it. I hate it. It feels like a coffin. Needles in my arm make me pass out now so it's good I'm laying down. I wish they didn't put a needle in my arm. I didn't used to mind. I didn't used to be claustrophobic. It's hard to go alone.

And who would come with me to just sit there in the room as I get slid into the coffin. No phones are allowed. They'd just have to sit there for an hour and be with me. Or read to me. Or tell me a made up story about adventures and I could be the hero; like the stories my dad used to tell us. And maybe hold lightly onto my leg so I'd know I'm not alone. But don't move. If you move, they have to start again. Don't move. Don't move. Who could understand that when I'm there, I don't want to talk. Or I do. Or I'm happy. Or I'm sad. Or I'm scared. Or I don't know what I am. And so just go with the flow and don't take it personally cause I'm the one who's sad or angry or whatever I am. Who would understand what I'm thinking.

I'm thinking -You can breathe in one hour. Just one hour and you can breathe. You can do this. Don't move.

My BFF Bryan Cranston totally gets me. Again, see Exhibit A and reference his views of my future as a host on SNL. He would totally come to sit with me for one of the MRIs if he wasn't so busy with his career. But I totally get that. He's a famous guy, with his own life to live and also, maybe most significantly, he doesn't know me. And perhaps he didn't say anything about my hosting SNL. Perhaps.

So anyway, I wear the shirt. MRIs are easier with the shirt.

I don't want to be defeated. I don't want to be scared. I want to be the one who knocks.

Chapter Forty-Three

Words and a Reminder

All of my life, I've been a writer. I have stacks and stacks and books of stories and memories and poems that I've written and recordings of stories I've created and narrated. When trying to process it all soon after I was diagnosed, I wrote a lot. I wrote a piece called "Words". I re-read it from time to time. And all this time, 6 years later, my feelings remain the same. Please read. Please see me. After all, this chapter has already been written.

Words

Tear stained page. No words yet. Just tears.

Swirls in my mind. Of words and thoughts too jumbled to make written sense. Words...

Flung about so casually. Flipping and flopping with no attention paid to their significance or damage. A fish on a boardwalk. No air. agony ignored, vain attempts for last breaths, of no relevance to anyone. Flinging about. meaningless.

Words.

meanings under-appreciated. unknown. impact not realized. So casually. Agony ignored. Vain attempts. Flinging about.

Words.

Diagnosis.

Realization.

Acceptance

=Surrender.

=Give in.

Acceptance...Surrender...Give in.

There can be no acceptance.

Be prepared to embrace, appreciate, be thankful for this new life; objectively labeled by all as mediocre at best. A crippled, brain numb fool at worst.

I will not. I cannot. I do not. Embrace. Appreciate. I am not thankful for...

Words.

Waiting. Expecting. Wishing against. Fingers crossed to be waiting for nothing. Nothing. The same. Keep it the same. But it will never be again. Because now I know what I may be waiting for and wishing against. How can any day be the same with this monster looming. Hovering. Blocking the sun. Blocking my sun.

Words.

Vitamin D is good for you! Magnesium is good for you! Dark green leafy vegetables are good for you! Keeping active is good for you! Getting enough sleep is good for you! Less stress is good for you!

These things- these good for me things- will they keep me from ending up in a wheel chair?

No.

Will they help my right hand work again?

No.

Will they help this disease subside, lessen.. this beast be driven to extinction?

No.

How are they good for me?

They are good for everyone!

I am not everyone.

Words.

Flinging about with no air.

What will drive this to extinction. I need to know.

But no one knows. Probably nothing.

Were that fish on the boardwalk a human in agony, gasping for air...would anyone notice.

Would anyone care.

My thoughts ache.

My feelings bleed. But these wounds can not ever by anyone be seen. There is no medication for them. There is no bandage or cast. For these cuts, there is no remedy to be found.

Words.

May 4, 2018 7 a.m. - You have brain damage. See it on the screen? Look at your brain damage. Here and here. Do you see your brain damage?

You have a lifelong, incurable, disabling, disease.

There is no cure. Hear me. Listen to my words. There is no cure.

I hear you. Every day. I hear you. Your words are inscribed on my newly found addle-brain. If I look I can see them etched next to the old damage. They are my new damage. New spots. New lesions. Your words. So casually spoken. Agony ignored. Gasping for air. Brain damage. Here and here.

Your infamous words live on. Eternity and beyond. There is no cure. I hear you.

I forget why I'm speaking. I forget where I'm going. I forget what I've done. I forget what I've seen. I forget. I forget. But your words live with me forever. I hear you. There is no cure.

Pain? Yes. Fear? Yes. Disability ? Yes.

Positive attitude. A MUST.

There is no cure.

I remember who I was. Will I always? I was smarter. I was more capable. I remember who I was. Will I look back on this writing with knowing sadness or will I look quizzically - wondering how these words ever found each other?

And who will my children remember. In visions of their childhood, who will they see. The then or the now, me.

I know the answer.

I see a woman in a wheelchair and a piece of me crumbles. Does she have what I have? Are we in the same club? Does anyone know her? Does anyone see her? She's in there but can anyone see her? Somebody must know her. Right? Did she believe there would be a cure? Did she eat dark leafy green vegetables? Her children. Did they see her fall? Over and over. Did they see her fall. Did friends tell her to get a cane, just in case she needed it. Seemingly aware of something she didn't want to believe herself. Did she know the moment when she became a liability to her children. Did she fear holding their hands crossing the street because she could fall and bring them down too. A liability to her children. How can she as a parent be at peace when she has become a liability to her children. The people she would protect with her own life over and over again. Now must be protected from her. Does she wonder how this can be true. That she could bring her children down. Does anyone know how her heart aches for her children.

Positive attitude. It's a must.

Get plenty of sleep. It's good for everyone.

Get a cane. Just in case.

Words. Flipping and flopping. Walked over and ignored.

I'm in here, in this ever developing world of solitary confinement, sentenced to life for no fault and no crime. can anyone see me. hear me. feel me. Wishing. Fingers crossed. An entree of smiles with a side of pain. Or is it the other way around.

Oh, and the chemicals. So many chemicals. You need to ingest the chemicals. For staying awake. For falling asleep. To cause cancer. For feeling too much. For feeling too little. To cause addiction. For breathing. For pain. For rotting your body from the inside out until you are no longer recognizable as anything but a cesspool of toxicity. To bandaid you now and destroy you later. That's what chemicals do. You know it and I do too Wait, let me get my prescription pad. Here's more.

Deeper and deeper I go into the cocoon of myself. Not through desire but through the seemingly natural evolution of the word "diagnosis".

Do you hear me? There is no cure. Look at the screen. See your brain damage? Here and here. Do you hear me?

Every day.

I hear your Words.

————---

So to you, my reader, I want you to know that your decision to read my book, has left me a little less invisible. I appreciate that. I thank you for that.

And before we part ways, I'll ask you once more to please remember:

I am not I

Pity the Tale of Me

Made in the USA
Columbia, SC
16 July 2024

38452353R00104